R & R

a sex comedy

E.M. Schorb

HILL HOUSE   NEW YORK

ISBN: 978-0-578-47471-7

ACKNOWLEDGEMENTS

Parts of *Resurgius* have appeared in the following publications:

The poem "The Naked Truth" first appeared in *The Lyric*.

The poem "O Popular Moon" first appeared in *Bitterroot*.

"The Mall on the Moon" first appeared in *The Potomac Review*.

for

Patricia Schorb

and

Selah Bunzey

and

Leslie Kell

who

like to laugh

RESURGIUS

A Sixties Sex Comedy

by

E.M. Schorb

RESURGIUS

*. . . to see one-half of the human race
excluded by the other from all partici-
pation in government was a political
phenomenon that, according to abstract
principles, it was impossible to explain.*

A Vindication of the Rights of Woman
—Mary Wollstonecraft

1

To Serge Bering-Strait, young ward of five aggressive, progressive, and, to him, oppressive, women, the phrase "Swinging Sixties," meant, at this moment, swinging like Tarzan from a subway strap.

But he was no Tarzan. His mother and four aunties had forced *him*, a *poet*, out of his Greenwich Village attic sanctuary and into the struggle for survival here among the *poloi*, where he felt in imminent danger of being crushed, which partly accounted for the look of angst he wore. But what really depressed Serge was that he had already missed a whole half-hour of reading from his beloved Plutarch's

Parallel Lives, which he gripped under his free arm, and which was being pressed painfully into his ribs by a grubby fellow traveler. The "lumpen mob" was just too thick this morning, too thick to hold up his book—so thick, in fact, that he was not sure if he had missed his stop.

There were no signs in prominent display, the windows were painted gaily over with spray paint, and the terrific, ear-splitting cough made by the loud-speaker hadn't served in the least to clear things up. Serge decided to get out.

The train doors shut just as he stepped through them, smudging the shoulders of his new London Fog, a twenty-third birthday gift from his Auntie Janet Hoover, and knocking his copy of Plutarch's *Lives* from his grasp. The book was kicked ahead of him into obscurity by the mob's stampeding hooves. The train reopened its doors with a snort, shot them shut behind him, and pulled away.

It was the wrong station. Well, it was a natural enough mistake. He had not had time to develop that sixth sense about subway stops that comes with practice. He had only been on the job for a few weeks, his Auntie Janet Hoover having procured his position as staff writer for him through her connection with the boss, the lady editor Bettina Battle, who sometimes worked for Auntie Hoover as a speech writer. Auntie Hoover was in politics, an assistant to Mayor Dimwiddy.

This was not his first job. His first job was being a poet, which he had been since his prodigious graduation from New York University some five years before, at eighteen. But Auntie Hoover thought that it was high time that the little "genius-boy" got out of the house. She thought his life up in his garret room was very unnatural.

When the crowd thinned, Serge found his battered Plutarch near the turnstile. He could have cried for the thousand indifferent kicks it had received.   A tasteless modern world had no respect for the classics.

A train roared in, with a long, shrill, metallic scream of the sort he imagined Jurassic raptors might have used to indicate their ravenousness.

Pressed into the center of the crushed subway crowd, which held him upright, levitated, feet adrift in space, arms bound to his sides, his Plutarch bruising his ribs, he could still get a sniff of fetid hot air from above; but the air-conditioning blew his inherently wild red hair askew and, when he opened his spectacled eyes, he was forced to look at the advertising signs over the windows. HEMOR-RHOIDS? one asked, distastefully. TAMPONS? another invited. UNDERARM ODOR? another challenged. JOCK ITCH! another asserted. THE NAKED TRUTH another— wait!

THE NAKED TRUTH?

Ah ha! The bureaucrats at the Poetry in Motion office had finally got around to putting up his subway poem—

THE NAKED TRUTH

The naked truth will lie.
I don't believe in facts.
What's in the inner eye
Is what the outer lacks.

The night's an Arab's sheet
Of swirling blue and black.
The earth is at his feet.
The stars are at his back.

And even love is true
If we should make it so.
O, lover, love me too!

O, lover, let me go!

by Serge Bering- . . .

The lights in the car flickered, went out. Serge thought of his loss of time. It seemed hours till they got started again, but it turned out to be only twelve minutes when he could read his watch.

The light turned green in Serge's favor and he stepped out from the curb, preoccupied with thoughts of his dreary, poetry-corrupting writing job, his guilty tardiness, when a taxi swerved in front of him with a screech, blasting its horn, the driver, a woman who looked as mean as Auntie Hoover, cursing him with words even more raffish than passages from Allen Ginsburg's horrible "Howl." As his eyes rolled back in his head, Mother Nature's eternal blue highway shone between the tall, artificial escarpments of skyscrapers, still, surprisingly, possessing the magic of modernity—and he saw, high above him, in that blue wonder, an airship shaped like a Frankfurter. It was the Quaint Wiener Balloon, the inescapable red hot dog that he saw in every store, at every stand; but this one was gigantic, so big that it outloomed the skyscrapers, seemed to even outloom the Goodyear *dirigible*!

QUAINT WIENERS

was written on its side, plain as day. And then, it floated out of sight, banned from the sky by the behemoth buildings it sailed over.

He entered the revolving door of the American Rubber Climax Building and was shot up sixty-nine floors to the offices of *Women's Omnibus* magazine. He got to work just on time but was immediately assaulted.

"Your 'food-on-a-stick' article is très—and I do mean *très*—putrid*,"* cried Serge's editor, Bettina Battle, sometimes known as the Battle of Britain, having arrived at *Women's Omnibus* from *Swinging London*, the magazine as well as the city.

"What's wrong with it?" Serge was shaking out his London Fog. He hung it on the clothes tree that took up valuable foot space in his cubicle. It was a sad, dripping sight. His Auntie Janet would sting with the insult of it. But then, Auntie Janet Hoover was always prepared to sting. He wiped his face and dried his glasses with tissue, superficially listening to Bettina Battle's cockney-inclined locutions while inwardly bemoaning the condition of his battered Plutarch. He had to pee.

"What's wrong with it?" Bettina Battle cried. "That's old shit! We want something new! We want new concepts! On the ball, Bering-Strait! On the ball!"

Serge could scarcely keep his eyes open. He'd been awake since two a.m. when the burglar alarm went off at Schlock's Delicatessen down the street from his mother's house. Since his air conditioner was on the blink, and his window wide open, he'd heard the alarm full blast. "New concepts," he ruminated. "Food-on-a-stick, just heat and eat."

"What's that?" cried Bettina Battle.

"What do you mean 'new concepts'?" asked Serge. "The stuff's a lot of dreck. Who'd eat it?"

"Bering-Strait, what are you saying?"

The din of electric Selectric typewriters and office machines seemed particularly intense. His head ached, and he had to pee, badly. He took a bottle of aspirins from his desk and walked to the water cooler with Bettina Battle in pestering pursuit. She eyed him ruefully as he choked down two aspirins.

7

"This is serious business, Bering-Strait," she said, while he strangled on the aspirins, repeatedly flushing them down with paper cup after paper cup of water. It was business, Serge admitted to himself, and the money involved made it serious, he supposed; but it was disgusting, nonetheless. He yearned for the classics. He even yearned for Jane Austen. If only Bettina Battle spoke to him like a character out of Jane Austen instead of sounding like the screeching flower girl in "My Fair Lady."

"You see, Bering-Strait, the mashed potatoes, ground beef, and peas are all smooshed up together into a ball, like a lollipop, and frozen on a stick. Then you pop it in the oven, and there it is, ready to eat! A quick meal for busy women in a busy women's world." Bettina beamed. "Isn't it wonderful? It's a new concept!" Now Bettina frowned.

"You've got to get serious, Bering-Strait. Magazines are in stiff competition with—I can hardly bear to say it— the telly, TV, the tube, say-screen, or whatever you want to call that monster."

"Say-screen?"

"Whatever—call the monster what you will—it's ruining our circulation. That's why we need new concepts."

"Won't it fall off when it's heated?"

"Won't what fall off?"

"The food off the stick! Won't it fall off when it's heated?"

Bettina looked at him, hard. "Uuum. You look beat, Bering-Strait. What's the matter, not getting enough sleep?"

"No, I'm *not* getting enough sleep," Serge said, yawning, "I was up all night. First a faulty alarm went off and woke me and my air conditioner's on the blink, and then I couldn't stop thinking about a novel I want to write."

"Novels are dead! Flicks and the Say-screen have already killed them. Do you want the monster to kill *Women's*

8

Omnibus as well? Here, we need people who can think on their feet around here—think original thoughts, new concepts," Bettina summed up. She stood looking at him, arms akimbo, waiting like a drill sergeant for a response from a recruit.

"Something like Amanda Quaint's idea for sky-mirrors?" Serge asked insinuatingly. Amanda Quaint wrote for a competitor of *Women's Omnibus*, *Ladies' Day*, and her recent article had caused a great stir among the New York magazine set. Leo Lerman had called her a genius.

"Quite, Bering-Strait, that's quite it! Think of it— constant daylight—'round the clock selling! Business would double. The world would have to run three shifts. Then too, it'd create a whole new market—sleeping aids; ear-plugs; sleeping pills; eye shades; black window curtains! Think of that, Bering-Strait! New concepts! By the way, I want you to get started on researching the new UNIVAC machine."

"The great computer that's going to revolutionize life as we know it?"

"I want the angle on what it'll do for women—help free them from low-paying office drudgery—"

Serge saw himself in his cubicle, wetting his pants.

"—elevate them to technical personnel, programmers and the like. See what you can bring out of the tin. I want some stats on women—proving their oppression. Up till now we've only had deductive reasoning to go by— observation. Now, with this UNIVAC III, we can get statistics to prove scientifically what we've believed all along, that we women are nothing but drudges and slaves for you men. The UNIVAC III will set women free!"

Serge asked, "Won't it just increase production, rather than freeing any workers?"

Bettina didn't approve of Serge's obvious lack of enthusiasm. "I've got my eye on you, Bering-Strait." She turned and marched off on stiletto heels.

Serge could not run to the lavatory, for fear of losing urinary control, but he got there as soon as he could. All the urinals were vacant, but Serge was urinal-averse. He went into a booth, sat down, and peed. His mother and aunties had trained him from a toddler to sit down when he peed in order to reduce splashing and mistargeting, or so they told him, taught him, and now it was impossible for him to stand and shoot. He washed his hands and went back to the office.

Serge spent most of the afternoon acquainting himself with his new assignment. He'd have to figure out the female angle on the Univac III. What would it mean to readers of *Women's Omnibus*?

At four-thirty, Serge begged to be unhanded by Bettina, who dragged him from his cubicle—where he had been racking his brains—and into her glassed-in corner office.

"Sir Gay . . ." she began, lighting a Virginia Slim, sinking into her swivel chair, and putting her amazingly long and shapely legs on her desk, spike-heels spindling articles that covered every aspect of women's life from hair-dos to toenail polish, from gourmet cooking to commodity investments ("How Women Can Make a Million in Pork Bellies").

"Serge!" he corrected. "Why do you always call me Sir Gay? You know that my name is pronounced 'surge' like the surge of the sea."

"Whatsum," Bettina said. "Thing is, I've had my eye on you for some time."

"So you said," said Serge, with a snip in his voice.

"You're a presentable young man in a pouffy sort of way, and I'd like you to escort me to a meeting of the Lunar Society in Greenwich Village tonight. *I* live in the Village and *you* live in the Village, so, after the meeting, you can see me home . . . or should I see *you* home? It'll be getting dark by then. I have a black belt in Karate, so you have no need to fear the mean streets of the Village after sundown."

Serge understood her sarcasm. The infamous nymphomaniac had been trying to get into his virginal pants since his first day on the job, but he had thus far managed to fend her off. She had gone from merely chiding him to outright bitchy persecution. Clearly, however, she was going to have another try tonight, taking a different tack. It was not that her beauty did not appeal to him, but that she had none of the sweetness his embarrassed virginity would require in his first lover. Her beauty was controlled by a harsh machine, a soulless battery, that energized a force field. In other words, she turned him off, but good!

"What's the Lunar Society?" he asked, trying to show polite interest.

"The Lunar Society is an association of professional women who meet monthly, and I am surprised, your mother and aunties being who they are, that you have not heard of it. *Our Mother is the Moon!* Doesn't that ring a bell?"

It did, faintly. A tiny tinkle. But, for as long as he could remember, he had been dragged to all sorts of meetings, conventions, and gatherings, yet, somehow, had managed, maybe, to have missed this particular one; or perhaps had actually slept through an earlier meeting of the Lunar Society, as he often slept through meetings, even sometimes snored through them. Sometimes all he had to show for a meeting was a bruised rib cage, where female elbows had poked him awake. His ribs were tender as a bird's.

"Why me?" he asked. "You can get anybody you want to escort you." But he already knew the answer. She wanted something new. Even a new disease would do for Bettina.

"Why must we go?" he asked.

"Because everyone who's anyone in the Women's Movement will be there. Don't you want to get somewhere in the magazine business? Well, you have to be inside. It's called networking. Besides, your whole family will be there. Now, no buts about it. Meet me at my limo out in front at five-thirty sharp. I have no more bloody time to spend on you. Not now. But I have something of great importance to tell you on the drive downtown." She pointed a long, ensanguined talon toward his cubicle, over the bobbing heads of busy, quietly desperate plebes. "Go!" she ordered, and closed the valves of her attention, as Emily Dickinson might have done.

At five-thirty sharp, Serge stood, like a reactionary lemming, a few feet in front of the revolving art deco door of the American Rubber Climax Building and refused to be moved by the outflowing crowd. Curiosity kept him in place. What was this thing of "great importance" that Bettina had waved before him like a carrot? And could he avoid the stick?

In the limo, a breathless Bettina Battle told him that she would be leaving *Women's Omnibus* poste-haste, for a better job, and that he might very well be her replacement as editor of the magazine. Her contract allowed her final choice for the editorship and her eye was on him, she said. "Yes, my eye is on *you*," she repeated, squeezing his thigh.

He giggled, squirming. Her thumb had plucked a funny string in his leg.

"Gawd!" she exclaimed. "You're skinny. I hope there is something a bit more hefty in that region. Shall we see?"

She reached out again, her fingers dancing like red-tipped spider legs.

"Yipes!"

To Serge, her offer of promotion seemed far-fetched, but curiosity kept him listening, as well as patiently struggling, almost arm-wrestling. But there was this little problem, eh? And so began a battle for Serge's honor in the back seat of Bettina Battle's limousine. His red suspenders were no match for her black belt. Putting a purr in her otherwise harsh voice, she whispered, "I hate these big macho muscle men. It's you cute little cuddly guys like Woody Allen I go for in a big way. You remind me of him."

She twirled his red and white polka-dot bow tie, and lifted her short skirt up to her creamy hip to show that she wore no knickers. There was a growling British lion tattooed on her hip with some writing under it. She started to lower the skirt but Serge stopped her.

"Wait!" he said. "What's that say?" And then he was able to read the legend: I'LL EAT YOU ALIVE.

"Good heavens!" Serge cried. He was appalled. He felt that any kind of tattoo or body-piercing was primitive, déclassé; simultaneously transfixing and stomach-turning.

"Hurry the bloody hell up," she cried, releasing her skirt to the grip of gravity. "It's a long dull drive downtown. Let's ball, baby!"

Her focus on the mechanics of unjamming his zipper had caused her not to realize that they had already arrived at the Village home of Hettie Freed, renowned author of *Men: The Feminine Mistake*.

Before Bettina could find a way to get his pants down, she found it necessary to make herself presentable. As she dabbed at her makeup, she said, "I never wear knickers, myself. I'm like the Boy Scouts—always prepared. I strongly suggest you heed my example next time. Get a pair of pants with buttons that button up. I can bite off a button."

She was miffed, but it wasn't his fault that she couldn't get his pants down, except for the struggling induced by his animal instinct for survival. He pulled his zipper up, then down, then up again, and it was free, and so was he. Silently, he thanked the jammed zipper heartily for protecting his terrified pee-pee, which seemed to shrink an inch back into his body at every touch of her long red talons. He pulled up his off-the-shoulder suspenders, got back into the jacket and London Fog she had fairly ripped from his back, stuck his Plutarch under his arm, and followed the Amazonian Bettina like a small, neurotic mutt on an umbilical leash.

The words "Hurry up, *Sir Gay*!" wafted over her shoulder on an ill wind, seeming to come from her tall French twist, as she climbed the steps of Hettie Freed's brownstone on Horatio Street, toward the networking delights of the Lunar Society's monthly meeting.

"My name is Serge, sounds like a *surge* of the sea!" he called after Bettina Battle, but she was not listening. The door swung open and she feinted a kiss on each dangling jowl of Hettie Freed, who asked who her little companion was. "This is Sir Gay Bering-Strait. You probably know his mother, Dagmar Bering-Strait—"

"—who invented bra-burning? Yes, of course I know Dagmar. She's here. I'm surprised I haven't met Sir Gay before this."

"My name is Serge. Like the *surge* of the sea," he insisted.

"*Gay* is quite an imaginative writer," said Bettina Battle. "He just finished a wonderful piece for *Women's Omnibus* on food-on-a-stick, and is even now researching the UNIVAC III machine for an article on its impact on the lives of women. He is a gifted journalist, so gifted that he

14

should never do anything else, and I'm quite sure he has no thought of changing to another line of work. He says he wants to write a novel, though. Am I right, Gay?"

Serge nodded in defeat.

"Sounds brilliant, darling!" said Hettie, patting Serge on the head. Out of politeness, he tried to wag his tail a bit.

"And you know who else is here tonight?" Hettie's grey jowls brightened with the blood of excitement. "That delightful new discovery who wrote the piece in your competitor's magazine about sky-mirrors—you know, so that no one can sleep. Oh, what is she called?"

"Amanda Quaint—yes," said Bettina, "I'm anxious to meet her."

Had Serge's mother introduced him to Hettie Freed, he'd have become the subject of a dissertation. Dagmar would have regaled Hettie with her favorite explanation for Serge's existence. "He was conceived," his mother would have claimed, "in a public swimming pool, and is the ward of the State of New York. Floating semen, you see. . ." And she would have gone into the long legal battle she had with the State.

The truth was that his father, Charles Bering-Strait, was dead, having died in a wine-soaked cardboard box behind the Port Authority Bus Terminal. His mother had rid herself of the "loathsome sex maniac" at an early stage of their marriage. Serge had once read a letter from his father to his mother that bore the salutation "Dear Furious," so he had some ideas of his own about their marriage.

He was certain that he had been named by his mother, not his father. He thought of the torment of his school days. Even the progressive schools that she had sent him to were torture chambers if you bore such a name as "Serge" and had been taught to sit down like a girl when you peed.

15

He followed Bettina Battle and Hettie Freed into the cavernous living room, acquired a glass of Dom Pérignon with little stars rising in it, and took two of the "Rosebud" wafers topped with darling little pink vaginas—someone mentioned that they had been baked by the up-and-coming feminist sculptor Judy Chicago—pregnant with Beluga, that he was offered, and from thence tried to become a wall-flower in a room full of aggressive kudzu—professional women of every size and shape.

From somewhere across the room, above the general uproar, he heard his mother's voice, a dentist's drill hitting metal, saying, "It makes me furious to think what these old-boy networks get away with. Look at the Masters in Augusta! No women allowed, my ass! Why, that mighty woman athlete, the great Babe Didrickson Zaharias could've whipped every one of those fat-assed, pot-bellied, dong-brained, male chauvinist pigs at golf or anything else. She could kick ass! It simply infuriates me. No women! They'll rue the day!"

Along with the Champagne and cookies, Serge had somehow acquired a flyer stating the purpose of this gathering. ". . . to make the old-boy networks rue the day. . ." he read, glancingly, " . . . to pay tribute to the Great Tallulah Bankhead, our Lunar Mother of the Month, who went about naked in the Twenties, fearlessly, sweeping men underfoot like so much trash . . ."

Occasionally, the donkey-eyed head of a male feminist floated by as if on a pike, wearing an enthusiastic rictus for a smile. Like himself, these poor souls no doubt belonged to some powerhouse of a woman. Then someone started chanting "Women power! Women power!" Serge recognized the plangent voice of his Auntie Hoover, "She-Who-Must-Be-Obeyed," she who subjected Serge's attic room, or garret, as he preferred to think of it, to random searches for any indicators of masculine mischief, such as "Playboy" magazines, jockstraps, or condoms, she who had driven him from his secret meditations, from his poetry, and out into the cruel world—a basso profundo whose notability in any crowd could only be outdone by his mother's cry of "FURIOUS!" *Her* voice was even more irritating to him than Auntie Hoover's. He could feel his heart screaming in his chest every time he heard it.

His mother, Hettie Freed, and Bettina Battle gathered around the gleaming pink piano—an extraordinary instrument, Serge now noticed, because its three carved wooden legs were those of a woman in high heels.

Hettie Freed asked for the crowd's attention. She told them that Janet Hoover had a few words for them.

"Clear the way!" Bettina cried, making a path to the piano for Auntie Hoover. Bettina liked to be close to power—her motto was: "It's valuable to have a wise companion, and wiser to have a valuable one"—and Auntie Hoover was a valuable companion.

Bettina had thrown her arm over Auntie Hoover's shoulder and was reluctant to release her, but was forced to do so as Auntie Hoover, tank-like, ground her way up the piano stool and onto the piano to address the room from the mount, so to speak. She stood like a mighty Maillol, arms akimbo, and waited for the crowd to recognize her position of authority. One member of the crowd did, immediately, and shouted, "O mighty woman, empower us all!"

"At each of our monthlies we gather to pay tribute to a mighty woman of the past. Tonight we are going to honor the great actress and free spirit, the late great Tallulah Bankhead. Hand me that poster," Auntie Hoover ordered, and a life-sized cardboard cutout with a bracing flap was passed up to her from the crowd. She stood it next to her, stood at attention, and saluted it. It was a cutout of the

17

naked Tallulah, done in the style of Augustus John, wearing only a string of pearls, along with other natural products of womankind.

"Some of you younger members of the Lunar Society might not know the great Tallulah, but for those of us who have battled long and hard for women's rights, this ballsy, outspoken dame, inventor of camp itself, has long been an inspiration."

"The naked truth," a female voice whispered in Serge's ear. He looked around but recognized no one in the crowd.

Serge leaned on a pedestal that held a bronze statuette of Atalanta determinedly piercing a boar. He squinted at the little face of the boar and thought that it resembled himself in its agony. Then his agoraphobic narcolepsy overcame him.

He fell asleep until his ribs were poked. How long he had slept he had no idea, but he woke to the tune of "The Battle Hymn of the Republic," only the words were those of the "Women's Anthem."

Glory, Glory, Hail Tallulah!
Glory, Glory, Hail Tallulah!
Glory, Glory, Hail Tallulah!
Her Truth comes marching on.

"Hip, Hip, Hooray!" shouted the crowd, which was uproarious now with inspiration and Champagne.

Auntie Hoover addressed the gathering, saying, "We must adopt Sheila Michaels's suggestion that we refer to ourselves as 'Ms.' No more prissy 'Miss' or downtrodden 'Mrs.'" She beamed to the applause this inspired.

"How do you say that?" someone called. "I see it here in the flyer. But it hasn't got a vowel."

"Screw the vowel movement," roared Auntie Hoover. "That's just a lot of masculine crap. Just shout 'Mizzzzzzzz' for all the world to hear and take notice."

"What would be the plural, do you think?" the voice asked. "Mize?"

"Screw plural!" shouted Auntie Hoover. "Screw vowels! Just don't screw men." She whooped and the others joined in.

"I saw by the look on your face that 'The Women's Anthem' inspired you," purred the same soft voice that had whispered "the naked truth" in Serge's ear. "You looked so lonely, standing over here by yourself, I thought I'd bring you a fresh glass of Champagne. My name's Amanda Quaint. I know who you are. You're Serge Bering-Strait, the writer. I've read a couple of your pieces in *Women's Omnibus*."

She was a foot taller than he and wore a Mary Quant mini-skirt; but, somehow, she didn't frighten him. Most of the women he knew did. Amanda Quaint's voice was soft, forgiving.

He took the stemmed glass from her fingers—such pretty, well-manicured fingernails, such a nice shade of pink—and looked up at her; but he only had two hands and found himself awkwardly in possession of two glasses, the flyer, and his Plutarch, all of which he began to shuffle, or, more nearly, juggle.

Amanda Quaint said, "Here, let me take that. Why are you reading Plutarch? Are you taking a course?"

"Of course not." He blushed at his timid, almost inadvertent pun. "Everyone should know the lives of these extraordinary Greeks and Romans. Their parallel lives. The Anabasis and Katabasis—"

"Yes, I know all about that," she said. "I think that's Xenophon."

"You do?" His admiration for her lifted another notch. She took the empty glass and the flyer from him and managed to make them disappear while keeping her big violet

19

eyes fixed on him. Her grace amazed him, her beauty gave him palpitations. "My name is Serge," he said.

"Yes, I know," she said.

"You're Amanda Quaint," he said.

"Yes, I know," she said.

"I'm sorry," he said.

"What have you got to be sorry for?"

He tightened his lips and shook his head. "I don't know. Sleeping on duty, maybe. I just feel sorry all the time."

"I didn't know you would be so shy," she said. "I read your beautiful poem on the F Train—'The Naked Truth?' Until this morning, I didn't know you were also a poet. A very romantic poet, at that! A little old-fashioned, but I like that. I like the old romantic poets much better than the Beats."

His eye-beams, through his horn-rims, rolled down to her open-toed pumps and back to her head, a crown of gold. He recalled Yeats's lines, "That only God, my dear, could love you for your self alone and not your yellow hair?"

His attraction for her was instantaneous, chemical, genetic, he might have said, as if they had been brought together from the ends of the universe by Mother Nature herself, as if she had always been there in his very marrow, though his body was much too small for such a woman to have got into. In short, it was love at first sight.

"I think you're just brilliant!" Amanda Quaint said. "Men with brains and sensitivity turn me on." Serge didn't like the phrase, "turn me on," but it sounded sweet coming from Amanda Quaint. When Bettina had said much the same thing, during the drive downtown, it had sounded ravishing, a vulture's voluptuous hunger.

Embarrassed, he blurted, "Benjamin Franklin said that a man's arm was just long enough to lift a glass of wine to his mouth," and drank off half the new glass of Champagne.

He was afraid to look in Amanda's eyes, for fear that they would not show responsiveness. "Quaint? Are you related to the Wiener King? I saw his balloon this morning."

"He's my grandfather," she said.

Serge looked up at the ceiling as if in search of the giant red advertising phallus. When he looked down, Amanda Quaint was gone.

Then he saw her being pulled off through the crowd by Bettina Battle. The angel of his desire was being kidnapped right out from under his wiener-focused nose.

Bettina had seized Amanda by the arm and dragged her off, kidnapped her from Serge, in order to offer Amanda double her current salary to join the staff of *Women's Omnibus*.

"We're looking for some new concepts," Bettina said, pulling Amanda away. "Sir Gay doesn't get it. He's a young fogey—never would have come up with an idea like your sky-mirrors."

"I think he's brilliant," said Amanda, "and cute, too."

"Don't get any ideas. That Nancy boy is my poodle. But, if you accept my offer—*entre nous*, I'm leaving to go into politics and the company is looking for a new editor—you might end up being his boss. Then he can be your poodle. But, listen, it's too noisy to talk in here. Come on outside to my limo. We can talk there. Bring your drink. Now what I want, darling, is for you to give two weeks notice to your present employer and join us at *Women's Omnibus* in a fortnit."

Bettina Battle had Amanda Quaint all to herself in her limo now. A signal from Bettina had set the wheels in motion.

"Wait!" cried Amanda. "I wanted to say good-night to Serge."

"Roll on!" Bettina ordered her chauffeur, and seized Amanda by the knee. "How would you like to replace me as editor of *Women's Omnibus* when I go on to bigger and better things? Eh, Sweetie, answer me that!"

Amanda lifted Bettina's hand from her knee.

"Bloody Hell!" cried Bettina. "If you don't learn a little flexibility, you'll never get anywhere."

"I'll take my chances," said Amanda. "And keep your hands off me, if you don't want this glass of Champagne ruining your makeup."

"Listen, lady, I have a Black Belt in Karate."

"Watch out someone doesn't hang you by it."

Bettina Battle looked ruefully at Amanda and roared again to her driver: "ROLL ON!"

Back at the meeting of the Lunar Society, Serge felt bereft by his loss of Amanda Quaint.

He felt like going home to his garret at the top of his family's house and having a good cry over a nice, romantic, melancholy poem—maybe something by Poe—say, "Annabel Lee."

But then he tried to look on the sunny side, as an old song encouraged. At least he had escaped being escorted home by the insatiable, black-belted "Battle of Britain." But having escaped "the Battle of Britain" meant that Serge was abandoned to the tender mercies of his mother and Auntie Janet Hoover.

2

By eight o'clock, they were walking the misty streets of Greenwich Village. His mother pinched his left ear. She was furious at something that he had inadvertently said at the Lunar Society. The tired tongue of his tired mind had tied the title "Mister" Freed to "Miz" Freed in his good-bye. Pulling on his ear was a nasty habit of hers. His ears were always red and sore from her gripping digits. From boyhood, he saw cauliflower in his future. And Auntie Hoover held his right hand with a rock-crushing grip. They lifted him over a puddle.

Auntie Hoover carried his scuffed Plutarch, at some point complaining about the state of the book's jacket and comparing it to the state of his London Fog, which, she reminded him, was her birthday gift to him.

She berated Serge for his carelessness, but he paid little attention, for he was used to being treated like a child by these two large and bullying women.

His mother agreed with his Auntie Hoover in her assessment of him. It made her furious, she asserted, *furious*, that he was still such an incompetent child. Fortunately, most of this washed right off his rumpled London Fog. He had heard it all before, and, anyway, nothing could erase the image, seen through his misty glasses, of Amanda Quaint's seven-inches-above-the-knee, mini-skirted form from his hormone-drenched brain, his post-pubescent, testosterone-soaked soul. Fecklessly, he tugged for freedom, but they were too powerful.

Serge had grown up in the Village, had lived in the same five-story brownstone on Bethune Street all his life. The house had been passed down from his grandparents to his mother and four aunts. The family had made its money in brassieres. "Uplift by Updike." The slogan alone had made them a fortune in the Forties. Serge did not fail to see the irony in this, since his mother was famous for bra-burning.

Serge came to recognize a number of ironies and oddities about his family as he grew up. His Auntie Janet Updike had married a man named Hoover, who had run away from their honeymoon, so it was said, the only residue of this vanishing act being Auntie Janet's last name. The other three sisters, Charlotte, Emily, and Annie, were ink-stained spinsters who ran Boadicea Press out of the ground floor of the five-story brownstone. Serge heard it bruited about that they had once tried their hand at show business, as a trio, but were no match for Motown, and surrendered quietly to a non-vocal lifestyle. Occasionally, while they worked, they harmonized such tunes as "There's No Business Like Show Business," but when noticing that Serge was with them, fell into silence.

He would have described them as taciturn, if asked. Like many other failed artists, they had turned to politics. Their purpose was not money but a passion for causes, activism, anarchism, and general intellectual mayhem. They were as clever at stirring the pot as the three Shakespearean witches. Boadicea Press turned out what they referred to as "edification for the masses."

Even his friends, most of whom were themselves from artistic, bohemian, or eccentrically rich backgrounds, teased him about the oddness of his family, and made common comment about the women being so big and him being so small, so undersized and frail, wondering to his face, often enough, as to whether he was adopted.

And then, by her maternalism toward him, some might have thought him to be the son of their Puerto Rican house-keeper and cook, had they not known that that was impossible. Because his young friends were almost sure that the crazy Hispanic drag queen who tended him with such devotion, could not have given birth. Or could he?

Even the family's living arrangements seemed odd to those visitors who ventured into the upper regions of the house. His mother and Auntie Hoover had rooms on the third floor, the three Boadicea aunties had rooms on the fourth, and Serge shared the fifth floor servants' quarters with Juanna Donna Lorca, the transgender who ambulated about the house in high heels and flamboyant female costumes and dominated their domestic life.

It was as if the sisters were trying to put the thought of a male—boy or young man—as far from their minds as possible, even if compelled to admit his existence. Sometimes he felt like Mr. Rochester's closeted first wife in Jane Eyre.

But now, as he traversed the rain-gleaming streets of Greenwich Village, his American Paris, on wobbly knobbly legs, he yearned for that hot little garret where he could at last be alone with his dreams of romantic love. Was Amanda Quaint to be La Belle Dame Sans Merci? Or was she as generous and open-hearted as he hoped, as her wide violet eyes would suggest?

As they approached the house, they saw that Juanna Donna Lorca and her twin brother Hector Alonzo de la Lorca were arguing on the sidewalk where a little group of neighbors and passers-by had gathered to watch, including his Boadicea aunties. The rubbernecking was understandable, even forgivable, considering the show the Spanglish twins were putting on.

Juanna Donna screamed like an excited cockatoo and Hector growled like an angry bear. The front door of the house stood open, suggesting that Juanna Donna had pushed Hector out of it and down the front steps, suggesting it because Juanna Donna was still pushing Hector away from the house, backing both of her straight arms with her considerable bulk. Everyone thought of Juanna Donna as "her," not "him."

Hector raised his fist and dropped it and raised it again and dropped it again, sorely tempted. "I don't wanna hit you, so stop pushing me," he said. "How would it look, me hitting a woman, because that's what you look like?"

"But it don't bother you to come here and ask a woman for money; it don't bother you that I've been saving all my life to have my dong removed."

"You are a disgrace to all us Spanish males!" cried Hector, who, except for his mustache and masculine garb, looked just like Juanna Donna, with his square, handsome face and short husky body. But there was another difference between them. Juanna Donna had had a nose job, giving hers a ski-slope tilt, while Hector's nose was straight and a bit flat, like a handsome boxer.

"It reflects on me!" Hector shouted. He looked imploringly at the onlookers. "This thing is my brother. Would you believe it? My *twin* brother!"

"But I will be your sister as soon as I save enough money! No longer will I be Juanna Donna, half man, half woman. Then I will be Doña Juannadonna, a true lady. But you will never be Don Hector because you are no gentleman, no hidalgo, no true caballero!"

"You drag queen!" shouted Hector. "The shame! The disgrace!"

"The shame of a man who only comes to his sister for money to pay gambling debts!"

The fortyish twins squared off and circled each other like boxers. Hector's cuff links glittered, as did Juanna Donna's innumerable bracelets. The ruffled train of her black and purple Bata de Cola flamenco gown swept the sidewalk, becoming a damp rag. Her mantilla, caught on one large earring, flew like a cape, and her pumps clicked on the sidewalk as she circled Hector. "Punch my knobs and I break you neck!" cried Juanna Donna, who had been taking hormones for years.

Hector paused to straighten his powder-blue tie, dropping his hands to do so, and Juanna Donna released a straight right to his chin.

"Son-of-a-bitch," he cried. "I didn't think you'd hit me. Look, everybody, I want you to know this is a man I am fighting with—a drag queen maybe, but a man just the same—and I have every right to hit back." And he did—right on the tip of Juanna Donna's ski-slope, Bob Hope nose.

"Now you've gone too far," shouted Auntie Hoover, stepping into the fray and walloping Hector left and right with Serge's Plutarch, a heavy if tattered tome.

While Juanna Donna and Hector were evenly matched, being twins, after all, Hector was no match for Auntie Hoover, who came at him like some kind of war machine, backing him up and finally causing him to turn and run from her onslaught, much to the amusement of the crowd, who hooted, cheered, and applauded. "Female assertiveness—" she said, looking after him, "macho men are no match for empowered women."

As if to emphasize what she said, the defective alarm of Schloch's Delicatessen down the street went off, sounding like a screeching banshee, and one could see from Hector's body language that it terrified him. He may have believed himself pursued by Auntie Hoover, a tank with a siren. He ducked into the sanctuary of the first bar in sight, Rocky's Rendezvous.

Juanna Donna felt satisfaction in her knowledge that Hector had entered a gay bar. The last laugh was on him. Schloch's alarm stopped screaming with a final gurgle, and peace was reinstated on Bethune Street.

In the house, in the kitchen, holding a hanky to her bloody nose, Juanna Donna said, "I hopes you no expect no food from me. I'm nobody's Sancho Panza. You Quixotes get yourselves some queki de limón, if you wants."

After checking Juanna Donna's nose and seeing that there was no real harm done, Serge's mother and four aunties busied themselves at the unfamiliar domestic task of making tea and serving themselves cake. They sat at the long kitchen table, like a group of irritated firemen just in from a chemical burnout.

"Put your head down between your legs," Dagmar advised Juanna Donna. "Isn't that a good cure for a nose bleed?" she asked Auntie Hoover.

Auntie Hoover said, "Boxers put their heads back." Auntie Hoover was a boxing aficionado. The three Boadicea Aunties devoured their lemon cake, making masticating sounds of supreme satisfaction.

No help from that direction.

Juanna Donna's eyes flashed at them. She pulled a bloody paper towel away from her nose and said, "Ain't any of you got normal female nursing instincts like Juanna Donna, whose brain has been marinated in estrogen? O.K." she added, "you're all testosterone titties, but then you could at least be gentlemen. A gentleman would help me. ¿Ya no hay nobles hidalgos ni bravos caballeros, who can protect us females? They have all left it to your Auntie Hoover to act like a real he-man, out on the street at least. But not in here!"

She watched in disgust as Auntie Hoover heeded nothing but cake. "You'll see," she cried, "I won't cook nothing 'round here for a week, and you all starve and see if I care. Some gentlemen, some true caballeros! Bad pipples, I say." She looked at Serge with disgust in her burning eyes.

"Bad pipples! I got to take care of my nose," she told him, as she staunched the flow of blood with a new handful of paper towels. "Oh, my God!" she shouted, "there's blood on my beautiful mantilla. I have wiped my nose with it. I have to soak it, queek." She headed for the upper regions of the house.

"I have an idea for a story about a brave caballero," Serge told her, following in her wake, "a real *macho* man. I've been thinking about it for some time and I'm going to call him Resurgius."

"What kind of name is that?" she asked, turning to him on the staircase.

"Dog Latin for a resurgent Serge, a comeback kid."

"Comeback from where?" she asked, still holding a wad of paper towels to her nose.

"From being pecked raw, Juanna Donna, that's where. Can I have a few of those peppy-steppy pills you're always popping when you clean? I'm going straight to my room and get started, and I need some pep. I've had a long, exhausting day, but, boring as it sometimes was, aggravating as it sometimes was, it was also inspiring, because . . . I fell in love today—love at first sight—and so, at last, I've got the heroine of my book to further my inspiration—someone to put on a pedestal and look up to; and I need my energy tonight; while it's all hot in my brain. Energy! I'm determined to get started right away. Right now! Tonight!"

Juanna Donna reached in her skirt pocket and filled Serge's palm with little red pills. "You can hop all night on these little red diablos," she said. "Once I stay up for a week. Remember that time when I cleaned the whole house and everybody get mad at me because I threw everything out? It was them diablos."

"But I'm afraid, Juanna Donna. I'm afraid I won't have the will or the energy to come home every night and work on this book. Writing a novel is a marathon. I'm just not sure I can maintain the discipline required. That's why I want you to do something special for me. I want you to promise me that you won't let me weaken, that you'll make me write every night, until I'm done, that no matter how tired I say I am, or how tired you think I am, you will help me to complete my task. Swear it!"

"Suppose I have to box your ears or throw a bucket of cold water in your face?"

"No matter what you have to do, just don't let me weaken."

"These I swear to, cross my heart and hopes to die. See, nothing crossed 'cept my toes stuffed in these pumps, but I can't help that. I will be your second will, I swear before God and Puerto Rico. Now, get busy! Hit those keys!"

Serge took the pills and went into his room. Soon the little red diablos made him feel as if he had a rocket in his brain. He was lifting off.

He stripped to his polka-dot boxer shorts and sat down at his desk.

Outside his open window, before which sat his broken air-conditioner, there was a God-like roll of thunder, and rain swished down from above in silver streaks like swords.

A breeze wafted in and his brain was alive, inspired. He wanted to bang out the title of his proposed opus in caps so large that the world could not fail to read them. But, disappointed at the size of the typed caps of his title, he took up a marking pencil and furiously printed across the top of the page and underlined—

RESURGIUS

3

"You look kinda droopy," said Bettina Battle. "I hope you've been burning the midnight oil on that UNIVAC article. How's it coming?"

"Oh, coming right along," said Serge, looking at her through bleary eyes and blurry glasses. She was barring the entrance to his cubicle and he imagined how a caged guinea pig must feel. She didn't even provide him with a nowhere wheel to run on. Bettina loomed over him like Wonder Woman about to lasso an evildoer. Her incredulity was tangible. She waited, threateningly, with the patience of a cat playing with a mouse, and Serge said, "Really, Bettina, it's going fine."

"It had better be," she warned, turning to scan the enormous room full of workers like a sniper seeking a target, beading in on one here and one there with telescopic and predatory phthalo-green eyes. Serge knew that further reference would be made. She turned back to Serge. "Have you given any more thought to my offer?"

"I thought about it most of the night. It kept me awake. I only had two hours sleep, so, if I look droopy, it's your fault."

"Come back to my office later if you need some Scotch in your coffee." As if in the throes of a drug-induced hallucination, Serge saw the mask of her face morph from iron warning to lascivious rubber invitation. He blinked in an effort to focus, then saw her toss him a wink as she went on to her next harassment, the object of which might be male, female, or potted plant.

He wanted to do as Juanna Donna had ordered and call Amanda Quaint, but he was very much afraid that she would reject him. Bettina Battle, attractive as she was, simply

31

turned him off. Her subdermal coldness and raptor-like aggressiveness made her seem anything but a beautiful woman. Rather more a bird of prey.

He wasn't often pursued by beautiful women. He wasn't often pursued by women at all—except for his mother and aunties, whose pursuit of him was like that of a riot squad. He remembered a love-struck stick-figure of a girl in grade school, and didn't a young woman once wink at him on the subway? Or had she caught a bit of dust in her eye? He had always preferred to think that she had winked. But it was a strange fix he found himself in, being pursued by a beauty who gave him the sinking sense of a green-eyed monster.

Now on the other hand, Amanda Quaint was easily as beautiful as Bettina Battle but radiated a tolerant kindness, "a glad kindness," as Yeats had put it in a poem, that, strangely enough, made him even more afraid of her than of Bettina Battle. Just what was this fear he felt? Well, he knew, didn't he? It was the fear of rejection. Why should such a lovely and decent young woman want a little skinny sack of bones like him? Bettina Battle would devour whatever was put before her, but Amanda Quaint was a woman of taste and discrimination—she liked his poetry—and so would fastidiously pick and choose.

He trembled at the thought of making the phone call that Juanna Donna had ordered him to make on pain of a spanking. How could he muster the courage? He must play the man, the he-man, the hero. He must be Resurgius! Fearlessly, Resurgius would pick up the phone and call.

Serge dialed for an outside line. He dialed the number of Amanda Quaint's office. When a voice came on the line, he said in his own cracked voice, "Amanda Quaint, please."

"Whom shall I say is calling?" said a quick New York accent.

32

"*Re-sur-gi-us*," he said, his voice cracking like a four-teen-year-old's. "No, no, no—I'm sorry, I got confused—tell her it's Serge Bering-Strait." And by this act of derring-do was actual magic in the form of electrical sparks produced on the line and the voice of Amanda Quaint poured like honey into his right ear, "Hello, Serge! I've been hoping you'd call me."

Oh, the wizardry of Edison! Faraday and Electricity! It was the voice of his beloved!

> *Mary had a little lamb*
> *Whose fleece was white as snow*
> *And everywhere that Mary went*
> *The lamb was sure to go!*

Was it the telephone or the Victrola? It was Edison, wasn't it? Serge was rattled.

"Is that you, Serge? Where are you?"

"_____"

Serge, for a hair-raising instant, could not speak. Then, his wild reddish hair settling on his head as after a bout with one of Tesla's electric arcs, he squeaked—

"Yes, yes, I'm here." And now so were the words—"I was wondering would you—could you—do you think we might—what I mean is—"

"I'd be delighted to meet you after work. Would you come over to Rockefeller Plaza and meet me? I'll be behind the statue of Prometheus. Shall we say sixish?"

"Abso . . . abso . . ."

"Absolutely," said Amanda Quaint. "I'll be waiting."

And true to her trueness, just as Serge Bering-Strait had known her nature to be honorable and trustworthy, there she was waiting behind the glistening, fountain-wet buns of the golden statue of Prometheus. Yes, Prometheus had brought fire and there she was, the flame in his heart, looking even more beautiful than he could remember, her blonde hair in a golden French twist, a white lace blouse tenting her ample bosom, her Mary Quant mini valancing unimpeachable legs, her pink-peeping open-toed pumps heeled five up, and, most striking of all, her violet eyes seeking him in the crowd that seemed to be sucking up all the air around him. How was he to speak to her without air with which to waft his words?

"Serge! I'm so happy to see you! Why do you look at me like that?" she asked, looking down at him. "Are you hungry?"

Hungry for the lips of my desire, Serge might have answered with Ernest Dowson's words but didn't.

"I'm famished," said Amanda, taking his arm and leading him hastily around to the front of the al fresco restaurant and down its steps. They were seated at a table from which vantage they could see Manship's bronze, gold-leafed statue of Prometheus stealing fire from the gods as a gift for humankind in all its full frontal glory. To Serge, it was the very vision of Resurgius, his hero. Behind Prometheus, the seventy-story RCA Building towered up and into cloud-piercing invisibility, the late sun peeling the skyscraper's façade, huge shadows wavering up its vanishing height.

The polyphonic chatter of countless voices, accompanied by the flappings of the flags of all nations, did not make their own words indistinct, for Serge and Amanda were focused on each other. Serge said excitedly, "I started a novel. Well, maybe it's just a novella—maybe it's going to be kind of short, I'm not sure. I guess it all depends on what happens next. It's going very fast," he rushed on, "now that I'm on to it."

"What's it called? What's it about?"

34

"The hero is named Resurgius, and he looks like that Prometheus, all golden muscles, not like me at all, and it isn't autobiographical like so many first novels. No, it's a work of the imagination. It's futuristic. But it's a love story, for sure. Resurgius is the kind of guy who never has to say he's sorry."

"But he'll say it if he should, won't he?"

"Sure, he's not afraid."

"Can I read it when you're done?"

"You'll be the first, Amanda, because I trust your judgment."

"Really? It's so sweet of you to say so."

The waiter brought them their drinks—a Whiskey Sour for Serge and a Screwdriver for Amanda.

"Cheers!" said Amanda. She put her drink down. "How exciting that you've begun a novel. I'm facile enough for articles, but I could never dream of writing a novel. But you—you being a poet—I bet the words just cascade from you."

"Well, sometimes they just dribble. But don't under-rate yourself," said Serge. "Your article on sky-mirrors is one of the things that inspired my novel."

"Really? How thrilling! But you know, I was assigned to write that article and, in truth, thought the whole idea was crazy. I, for one, like to sleep at night. It's plain nutty! Just another way of getting more work out of us poor peons."

"Gee," said Serge, "I thought there was something romantic about it."

"That's what I mean about you," Amanda picked up enthusiastically, "like all real poets you see romance in everything. You have a romantic heart. That's what I love about your poetry—

The night's an Arab's sheet

Of swirling blue and black.
The earth is at his feet,
The stars are at his back.

Oh, it gives me goosebumps! Did anybody ever tell you
that you look like a skinny Dylan Thomas? All that wild red
hair, and that cute little bulbous nose. If only it were red,
too, then you'd look just like him, but I don't suppose you
drink enough."

"I had three Whiskey Sours in a row one night!"

"*Did* you? Well, I really wouldn't want to be friends
with a boy who drank too much, even if he was a poet."

"I'm only going to have one—now."

"After we eat, shall we take a walk?"

"Where to?"

"Oh—uptown—maybe up to Central Park. It's such a
beautiful early autumn evening. I love autumn, don't you?"

"Oh yes," Serge said. He would have loved anything
that she loved. For he loved her more each instant that they
were together.

"Tell me about yourself," Amanda said later, as they
joined the flow up Fifth Avenue, toward Tiffany's and on up
to the Plaza Hotel and Central Park. He had to reach up to
hold her arm, his thin fingers gripping a solid bicep. The
power of her beautiful body thrilled him.

"I'm twenty-three years old," he said, "and a graduate
of N.Y.U. School of Journalism."

"What's your family like?"

"Women."

"What?"

"All women. I have a mother and four aunties."

"Oh, yes, I know who your mother is, and I know your
Auntie Janet Hoover. They're famous in lib circles. You
say you have three other aunts?"

"Yes. Charlotte, Emily, and Annie. They run Boadicea Press."

"Oh, we all know Boadicea Press. I read a number of their books when I was taking Women's Studies at Harvard. Let me see . . . there was *The Tyrannical Male, Football Wives,* and *Beaten Down and Beaten Up.* Those are a few of the titles I remember. Personally, I think they're a little extreme. I have a grandfather, a father, and three brothers who are almost as sweet as you are. I don't think we have to defame the whole male sex just because of the misbehavior of a few."

"That's my point," said Serge enthusiastically. He was almost swinging by her arm and tap-dancing as he tried to turn and look up at her. She took such long strides. Strident, that was her walk, strident—but she was so sweet.

"That's my point exactly," Serge repeated, "that you don't defame a whole sex just because you've got a mad on at a few members of it. Men say derogatory things about women, too, but they're doing the same thing. They're stereotyping. They're not trying to understand. I try to be fair-minded."

"As do I."

"I can tell. A lot of women don't, though, don't try. A lot of women just think men are no good, especially nowadays, with the Women's Movement in full swing. Wow, I grew up seeing the whole thing from the female point of view. The only masculine point of view I got at home was from Juanna Donna, who is more of a woman than a man, at least nowadays. On the other hand, I hardly knew my mother—hardly *know* her. My real mother, the mother who raised me—well, I know it sounds crazy—has been a transexual man who was much more maternal than my birth mother."

"My goodness! Tell me about it."

"Well, Juanna Donna's our housekeeper. She even taught me Spanish, or, what you might call, Spanglish, a mixture of Spanish and English. Juanna Donna came from Puerto Rico just about the time I was born and got a job as our housekeeper and really became my nanny, although in those days he called himself Juan de la Lorca, or so I've been told. He calls himself Juanna Donna, nowadays, and, to tell you the truth, I've always called him—or her—that, and I'm not a bit sure what his real name is, really. I'm pretty sure her last name is Lorca, though, like the poet."

"Garcia Lorca?"

"Right. But she'll always be Juanna Donna to me. I think I named her that when I was a kid and everybody started calling her that. But Juanna Donna's no poet." He put a hand on his heart. "Poet or not, male or female, she's like a mother to me. Sometimes I think the male can have more maternal instincts than the female, at least that's been my experience—and bigger boobs!"

"There's truth in what you say," said Amanda. "I bet you'd make a wonderful father. Even now, I'm writing an article on the more extreme forms of feminism, which I call—the article, I mean—'Have Some Feminists Gone Too Far?' It poses the question whether a small group of libbers—and remember, I consider myself a serious libber—want social equality—equal pay, for instance, for equal work, or actually want superiority; whether we want—or should I say *they* want—loving relationships with men or no men at all. At times it seems as if the latter is the truth of the matter.

"Take the case of Valerie Solanas, the founder and only member of S.C.U.M., the Society for Cutting Up Men. I've read something she wrote and it's absolutely insane. She sent me a manuscript, hoping, I guess, that I had some pull and could get it published in one of the magazines. I was free-lancing at the time. Poor thing! She's bound to wind up doing herself or someone else some harm. We libbers are not all like her! I don't like the idea of some women speaking for other women. We're independent thinkers, each and every one of us, or should be."

"How wonderful!" cried Serge, bouncing along beside her, enthralled by her words, only vaguely aware that they were approaching Fifty-Ninth Street and Central Park South, walking just to be walking and talking—"Because my novel is a spoof on the very extremists of whom you speak. I try to keep it amusing, but thinking of them can still hurt a fellow."

"That's because you're a poet and are highly sensitive," said Amanda, "but you mustn't become bitter. There's so much sweetness in life and you must try to focus on it."

"Oh, it's O.K.. I haven't the strength for much bitterness."

"But you must keep your spirit up. You must not slump."

"I stand erect when I'm with you."

"That's quite a compliment. Look," Amanda cried, "we've walked all the way up to the Hotel Plaza. Look," she cried again, excitedly, "the Hansom cabs are waiting across the way. Shall we go for a ride through the Park?"

"Amanda, my dear, they are not Hansom cabs, no matter what they tell the tourists. A Hansom cab has two wheels, seats two people, and the driver rides in back. You must have seen them in a Sherlock Holmes movie. These are four wheeled carriages and the driver drives from the front. See that fellow?"

"Yes, I see what you mean." She laughed, "You certainly have a didactic streak in you."

"I'm sorry," he said, "I'm always trying to get things straight in my own mind. But that fellow!" He pointed to the first carriage driver in a queue of carriages. "That carriage driver is Juanna Donna's brother, Hector."

"How interesting," said Amanda.

"That's Juanna Donna's *twin* brother."

"That's her twin? He doesn't look a bit feminine to me."

"Juanna Donna has had her nose done and has been taking hormones for years. She has boobies and wears dresses, the fancier the better. I guess you could say she's left her twinship. This was probably how she looked when I first knew her but I can't remember that far back."

"He looks very macho . . . except for the love beads."

"Yes," said Serge, "that's something different."

They had approached within a few steps of Hector's carriage and Hector had recognized Serge and called out, "Sergey, qué passe? Are you come up here to take the beautiful lady for a ride through the park?"

Hector jumped down from the carriage. He was wearing a top hat and carried a buggy whip. "Please meet my wonderful old horsy, Hidalgo, a true gentleman." Hearing his name, Hidalgo turned his grey head toward them, fixed his big brown eyes on them, and whinnied. He looked old and tired and patient.

"What a sweet animal," said Amanda.

"Allow me to introduce myself, Señorita—Hector de la Lorca, at your service," at which he bowed to Amanda.

"This is Señorita Amanda Quaint," said Serge.

"Enchanté," said Hector, bowing again. He said, "It's best in French."

"Enchanté," Amanda responded.

"You are taking the señorita for a carriage ride through the park, are you not?"

40

"Oh, let's do," said Amanda. "It's so romantic."

The lights in the buildings all around them were coming on, one at a time and then in clusters. It was almost musical, the way they would run vertically or horizontally or then in a whole block of fifty or more windows, like the tentative beginnings and then the first full riffs of a symphony. Da-Da, Da, Da, Da, Da! And the tiny twinkles of the night lights in the darkening park could be seen across the way like lightning bugs.

"Will there be a moon out tonight?" Amanda asked Hector.

"When you get in the park the moon will be clear as a golden bell in the sky." He took her arm and helped her into the carriage. "If the señorita would not mind waiting for a moment while I speak to young Serge." And he turned to Serge, took his arm, and led him a few feet off from the carriage.

"Serge, my young friend, true son of my sister Juanna Donna Lorca, it has occurred to me that you might take pity on someone who is, after all, almost a member of your family, by blood, which is thicker than water, that you might consider helping me in my time of great distress."

"Well," said Serge, surprised by such a turn, "what can I do for you, Hector?"

"I have a gambling debt, so I borrow money from some people down on the docks who say my carriage and Hidalgo will be collateral for the loan. But the interest on the loan goes up so fast that the carriage and Hidalgo will not cover it. I ask them then what would happen if this should come to pass, and they say that I have knees, don't I? By which I think they mean I will be harmed. If I could get them the money before the interest goes too far, this would save me bodily injury. Enough money would save my poor old Hidalgo and the carriage. As you know, I went to see

Juanna Donna to ask her for help, but you saw what happened. She hit me."

"But, Hector," said Serge, "she is saving all her money for the big operation. You know what I mean. You know how important that is to her."

"To become a woman," said Hector sadly. "I know. But I am thinking when I see you, maybe out of your deep and abiding love for who is really like you mother you will help you uncle to set himself free of this terrible trap he is in."

"How big is this trap?"

"Fifteen Hundred Yankee Dollars would free Hector from a terrible fate."

"Fifteen Hundred Dollars! That's a lot of money, Hector."

"But you make good money, no? Is not so much for you, eh?"

"They really mean to hurt you?"

"They really mean to hurt me!"

"I have some savings," said Serge. He took out his checkbook and wrote Hector a check for what he needed to get himself out of trouble. He handed it to Hector. "You must promise me, Hector—no more gambling!"

"No more gambling, Señor! But you must promise me, please, please do not tell our Juanna Donna that you have lent me this money. She would be very angry. Now," said Hector, his voice lightening with relief, "I shall take you for the best, most romantic moonlight ride through Central Park that anyone has ever taken, with my compliments and Hidalgo's, at which Hidalgo turned his old gray head toward them and said something indecipherable and, no doubt, in equine Spanglish.

Hector kept Amanda and Serge in the park for hours (over two hundred dollar's worth of ride, gratis), a great,

42

stretch-marked moon overhead, pointing out places of interest like the Wollman Rink, the Sheep Meadow, the Pond, the Zoo, and the Carousel, and considerately falling silent and almost invisible when they came to dark stretches under cover of the leafy trees, the short dark tunnels, and the glowing high-arched bridges where he expected they needed privacy for petting and for the suction-cup snap-release of kisses, which he could hear between the clops of Hidalgo's echoing hooves.

They emerged from the park after midnight, drawing up before the splendiferous doors of the Plaza Hotel. Parting is such sweet sorrow, the Bard had told them both, and so, with one last kiss and reaching arms they said farewell. Amanda hailed a cab. Serge found a subway. Each dreamed of the other on the way home. At the stable on Tenth Avenue, Hector gave Hidalgo a cube of sugar and kissed him goodnight.

At home, Juanna Donna had waited up for Serge.

"What is the idea of coming in so late? How you gonna write tonight?"

"Oh, but I really want to write tonight! I have so much to say. My heart is full! Give me some of those little red diablos and dame una café, por favor—con leche! I'll write all night and believe me, Juanna Donna, I'll work all day tomorrow and feel like a new man, sans sleep, sans everything! I am inspired because I'm in love!" After changing into pajamas, bathrobe, and slippers, he sat down at his Olympia and began to conduct his symphony.

Coming up the stairs with a tray of coffee and a demitasse of little red diablos, Juanna Donna could hear the typewriter in action, like a syncopated clock.

43

4

39 Whitehall Street. So long as the Viet Nam war raged on, that infamous address struck terror into the heart of every young pacifist who was registered for the draft in the New York City area, and Serge Bering-Strait was no exception. A vaccine could prevent polio, but there was no way of being vaccinated against the draft, an epidemic that led to the crippling horrors of boot camp and perhaps even to death. And now Serge had been struck down in the very blossom of life. He dropped the brown government envelope and wobbled down the hall from his room to Juanna Donna's room on afflicted legs. Thought was beyond him. Emotions, like a thousand stampeding cows, crushed reason under hoof. Instinct alone sent him to Juanna Donna, a terrified child to his mother, to his Madre/Padre, to be taken to her ample, estrogenized bosom and held in hirsute safety.

"There, there," said Juanna Donna, "you mustn't be afraid, leetle Serge," and she rocked his tearful being in her arms. "I saw that nasty envelope when I took in the mail this morning and I knew right away what it was. Maybe I should have called you at work. But I was thinking maybe he wants to be macho about this, maybe he wants to act like that superhero he's writing about . . . what you call him?"

"Resurgius," he sobbed.

"Si, Resurgius! But I know that a writer is different from a hero"—she patted his hair, pushed it back out of his eyes—"and Juanna Donna Lorca, she cry too. She cry all morning, but then she get the idea how to get you out of this if you want to get out of it."

Serge stepped back and looked at Juanna Donna, his tearful blue eyes flashing with hope. "How? Quick, how? Tell me before my knees buckle!"

"I know you are my proud leetle nooky man, but you must pretend to like other boys. You must pretend, my leetle macho niño, to be almost as gay as Juanna Donna," and she flourished her fan, cling-clanging her bracelets. "I know lots of gays who want to get in and they pretend to be straight, so you don't want to get in, you pretend to be gay. Simple, eh? You know me all your life. If I had started my hormones when you were leetle, I would have suckled you. Just act like me and say what I would say. I show you how."

The brown induction envelope with the voice of authority emanating from it ordered that Serge bring toothbrush and toilet articles to the Armed Forces Induction Center at 39 Whitehall Street on a Friday at 5:30 A.M. Early September had been unusually warm, summery, but now autumn had set in and a cool breeze flowed into the car from the open window on the passenger side. Juanna Donna drove, chattering away to keep Serge's mind off where they were going.

Bettina Battle had been informed that he might not appear at work that day—or, for that matter, a long time into the future. Serge had called Amanda Quaint as well. She had assented to write to him as soon as he could send his address—just in case anything went wrong. No "Dear Serge" letters, she promised. His mother and aunties had decided on protest and had left the house at three A.M. bound for Peter Minuit Plaza where a number of celebrities were expected to gather, placards and megaphones in hand. Old Beats, young Hippies, and Flower Children were out in full pacifistic force, carrying "Make Love, Not War" signs and chanting "Hell no, we won't go!"

Juanna Donna, wearing a long, multi-colored serape, jangling earrings, and made-up to look like a Ma Jode who had struck it rich, came prepared to join the protest. She found a place to park, some distance from the Induction Center, and they walked the rest of the way, soon finding themselves in the midst of protesters and mounted policemen. Among the protesters, in the twilight morning, Serge saw Doctor Spock of baby book fame, several actors whose names he couldn't place, and the bearded Beatnik poet Allen Ginsburg, who wore an orange batik shawl, a huge flowered tie, a rosary, and a Buddhist amulet. There were cymbals on his fingers, of the sort affected by Egyptian belly-dancers.

"I'm gonna get me some of those," said Juanna Donna, pointing at Ginsburg. "Now you remember what I tell you," she said, letting go of his hand like a mother sending her child off to kindergarten on the first day. He waved to his own mother and aunties, but they were too involved in their chant of "Hell no, Serge won't go!" to notice him as he entered the faded nine-story red brick building of 1886 construction with barricades like vampire's teeth at its mouthing Moloch-like entrance.

He was no longer Serge Bering-Strait, but one of many, as he stepped through an elevator door that bore the slogan "The Security of World Peace Starts Here." Soon he was stripped for his physical, during which brutal military medicos subjected him to a number of dehumanizing indignities, such as having him bend over while they stuck their rubberized fingers up his ass and felt around. It was horrible, but why hadn't he had those medical fingers up his ass when he needed them to make the required weight, which he failed to make by about a finger's worth—they had him stuff down a bananna and that qualified him—and yet it put him in the mood for Room 604, the psychiatrist's office.

Now he did as Juanna Donna had told him to do. He tried to behave like Juanna Donna, queen of high camp. He rolled a thin, feminine shoulder at the shrink, flirtatiously, and said, in an unnaturally high-pitched voice, "Hi, Big

Boy," the very words Juanna Donna had told him to use. It wasn't easy, and it turned him red in the face, but still he said it, mortified, desperation being his king—or his QUEEN—at this most embarrassing moment. It was a question of do or die, so he did.

But what most injured his pride was that the shrink showed no doubt. "Gay," he said, with complete indifference. "Take this paper and go," and he stamped something on the paper. Serge felt as if the shrink had stamped "Gay" on his forehead.

When he left 39 Whitehall Street, a free woman—he meant MAN—relieved, happy, and ashamed, he saw his family being hauled off in a police van. Oh, well, it wasn't the first time that they had been hauled off in a Black Maria. But he had no one to tell that he had escaped the clutches of the military, death in Viet Nam, the end of Resurgius, the end of Amanda Quaint. Juanna Donna had been taken away as well and he had no way to get home because he could not drive, and, if he could, had no keys to the car anyway and so he must walk through the streets of lower Manhattan, the fingernail tip of the island, where no bar was open yet, and find a subway station. But where to go? It was still too early to go to work at *Women's Omnibus* in the American Rubber Climax Building—he shivered at the thought of rubber fingers adroitly invading his sanctum sanctorum and squeezed his pained self shut at the bottom—up tight though he may seem—and there was no one at home, his family by now, no doubt, behind bars, almost certainly singing, "We shall overcome."

The day grew light as he wandered, and, as he wandered, he wondered if he had done the right thing. He was distracted from his ruminations when he looked up at the early morning sky and saw the huge, familiar, still lighted wiener hovering overhead. The lights blinked on and off, reciting the mantra QUAINT WIENERS—*QUAINT!*—Oh, Amanda!—in many colors and in a fabulous syncopation. He only wished for Amanda's sake that he could be more like his hero, Resurgius, but, as Juanna Donna had said, a hero is one thing and a writer is another, seldom the same.

In Battery Park, he sat down on a dewy bench to give himself some horizon therapy, but the Statue of Liberty loomed before him and, like all women, fixed his attention. Now she was a proper mate for Resurgius, he thought, big, beautiful, and stalwart, leading the way with her torch, book in hand. Yo, Mama!

He could see Resurgius following her in adoration, as he would follow Amanda Quaint. This was Friday and, on Monday, Amanda might start work at *Women's Omnibus*. He would see her all day every day from then on. O joy! And O joy, too, because he was free of the government! It did irritate him that the minions of government so readily believed him when he told them that he was gay. Then he wondered if they knew what they were doing—if they saw in him something that he didn't know was there. He was an aesthetic type of person, even a bit prim perhaps, yes, rather pale and prim and thin and proper; but no, he was mad for Amanda Quaint, so he couldn't be gay. What it was, was that Juanna Donna had so well instructed him as to how to act, and Juanna Donna was an expert on both sexes. Well, enough of that! It was the government that was crazy, calling him gay, not Juanna Donna.

The phone rang and rang. Standing in his cubicle, holding the receiver, Serge realized there was no one at home yet. Probably all still at the police station. He was anxious to let them know that he had escaped the military, especially Juanna Donna, who would be a happy little mother to hear it—a mamacita.

"New concepts!" cried Bettina Battle, her lower lip waving a spittle-stuck Virginia Slim cigarette like a baton. Serge could see and hear her vividly from across the enormous office which faded around her. He was no more than seated at his Selectric when she was upon him.

"Where's my UNIVAC III piece? I could have written the damn thing myself by now. HOW UNIVAC WILL CHANGE WOMEN'S LIVES. Statistics Prove Women Superior to Men Any Old Day of the Week. Roll out the stats! What's the matter with you, Bering-Strait? You little twerp, you great twit! By the way, you're late! What's the meaning of dragging your skinny bum in here at Nine-fifteen?"

"I was almost drafted," he said. "Don't you remember? I told you I had to report for induction this morning."

"Well, when are they taking you?"

"They don't want me," he said, actual tears welling up in his eyes.

"Why not? Is there more than appears the matter with you?"

"I have a physical problem."

"What? Can't get it up? No balls? No dick? You certainly keep it zipped up!" She shouted so that the whole office could hear.

"Flat feet," he said, mortified.

"Flat head, more likely. New concepts come out of heads shaped like rockets," she shouted. "New concepts are ejaculations from erected heads. New concepts come like cum! Let me hear those fingers make music on that Selectric. I want to hear Mozart's Third Divertimento for the UNIVAC emanating from within your cubicle in five minutes."

She tugged the stuck Virginia Slim from her lower lip, waving a little spot of blood that dribbled down her chin vampirishly. "Hit those keys!" she cried, spraying tiny blood spots on his shirt. In a second he could hear her some distance away using the lash of her tongue on somebody else. He could hear the poor victim screaming inside his or her head, another lashed oarsman on the great pulsing trireme called *Women's Omnibus*.

Before he could write "Statistics show . . ." he was summoned to Bettina Battle's corner office. She leaned back in her pink padded swivel chair, another Virginia Slim stuck to her lip, her long legs and spiked heels up on her desk, and gave him a girlish smile as he entered. He closed the glass door behind him.

"Got anything on that . . . what is it you're working on?"

"UNIVAC. Statistics. Women are superior . . ."

"Got anything on that yet?" Her voice was soft and oleaginous.

"You just left me two minutes ago. I've hardly had time to get the paper in the machine."

"Sit down, Bering-Strait—Gay! Was I a bit harsh on you? I mustn't let anyone in the office see that I have favorites. You can understand that, can't you? You're not still crying, are you?"

"That wasn't about you. Just nerves from the Induction Center."

"Oh, that's right. You were drafted or something—or was it that you were not drafted? Wait a minute. Let me sort it out. I know—you were not drafted because you have flat feet, right? But there's nothing else wrong with you, is there?"

"No, I'm fine."

"A little slow, maybe, eh?"

"I have an I.Q. of 168."

"But that's in male terms. That would only be about 68 in a woman. Still, you're a cute little fellow, and I've decided to take you to a play tonight. What do you think of that, hah?"

"I'm awfully tired already. I had to get up at three o'clock this morning to go in for induction."

"Say, isn't there some way we can use that as an advertising concept? Write something up and show it to me. MEN DRAFTED BY REASON OF INFERIOR INTELLECT. Something on that order. Now, about this play—it's called 'Oh! Calcutta!' and the actors take off their clothes in it. Wobbling breasts and dangling dongs all over the stage. Definitely a new concept. Eliminate the story and give us the naked truth. That's all people want anyway. They really want to go about sniffing at each other's rear ends like dogs, so let's get to it. This should put an end to all that old fashioned talkie trash that Tennessee Williams and Eugene O'Neil write—and Shakespeare, my own countryman, he's the worst. Don't you agree?"

"I like Shakespeare," said Serge tentatively.

"Yes—but naked! To be naked, or not to be naked. That is the question. Sometimes costumes help, I admit, though. As your poem puts it, 'The naked truth will lie. The night's an Arab's sheet,' and all that shit. But a good looking bum is always a turn-on. What's a sycophant, Serge?"

"An ass-kisser."

"Even better, a brown-noser. That's what I mean about new concepts, Serge. New concepts! The world will never get anywhere without new concepts. I'll pick you up in my limo outside the building at closing time. Do you agree? I warn you, put a sock in your cake hole." She slammed a hand on her desk.

51

"Well that's settled. But remember, if you stand me up, I'm going to be very hurt. It's likely to bring out the bloody wrath in me." She winked, but Serge knew she meant business, and he couldn't afford to be fired just when Amanda Quaint was coming to work there.

"Of course I'm only ragging you, Serge. You know that, don't you, my little poodle? What, do I see more tears? Stop thinking about that nasty old Induction Center, will you? You're a free man now, no more Royal Marines. I've slept with all of them. Not a real man in the lot. O.K., buzz off and get me those stats! Oh, and that other thing—what was it?"

"An advertising concept from the Induction Center."

"Right! Find a product—food-on-a-stick for instance—and have all those naked inductees eating it while the doctors stick their rubberized fingers up their bum holes. You see that—I can come up with a new concept just like that," and she snapped her fingers, then pointed at the door. "Out, out, brief candle," she commanded, "I'm feeling conceptual."

While he worked, Serge constantly reminded himself that Disraeli had said that there were three kinds of lies; white, black, and statistical. He tried to shape UNIVAC's results to suit Bettina Battle's concepts, nodding off occasionally into the land of Resurgius where he was king. Once he ripped a cigarette from Bettina Battle's lower lip and she bled to death, but something happened and he ended up saving her by pressing his shirt tail to her lip like a pressure bandage. She opened her eyes and kissed him in gratitude; but no, it was not a sweet or grateful kiss, it was a lascivious kiss, filled with a viper-like tongue, and he tasted blood and venom. He pulled away and Bettina screamed, "You swallowed my Virginia Slim!"

That woke him. There they were again, the statistics;
but thankfully the wall clock, based on Greenwich mean
time, told him it was time to go home—oh, no, not home!
He had to meet her outside and go to see "Oh! Calcutta!"
Well, at least the Eden Theatre, where it was playing, was in
the East Village, close to home. He picked up the phone
and dialed home once more. Juanna Donna's breathless
question whistled in his ear.

"Did it work? I knew it would! We was all released
right away. You hurry home now. We waiting for you. We
celebrate your freedom, yo! Land of free, home of bravo!"

Serge told Juanna Donna he had an assignment.
Bettina would not take no for an answer. But he'd be there
as soon as the play was over. He promised.

Bettina was in a kittenish mood when he got in her
limo. She held out a Martini to him—there was a bar in the
car—and he took it from her and sipped it until she plunged
her long red fingernails into it—God knows where they had
been—to retrieve the olive. Then he could no longer touch
it. She snuggled close to him and he fell asleep and then she
shook him and he woke up. They were outside the theatre.
She took his hand and led him into the theatre, led him to
their seats, sat him down beside her and seized his arm in
both of hers, cuddling it. "Poor little dickey-bird," she whispered, "you must be exhausted."

He nodded, his eyes closed beneath his office stickum
spectacles. She said, "I want you to pay attention to this
play. I want you to review it." He opened his eyes to a
group of naked actors and actresses prancing about on stage.

"I want you to review their bodies—do a John Simon
on them, every crack and dimple—every stretch mark and
wimple. If you look closely," Bettina went on, "you can see
that every one of them has different colored pubic hair. I

want you to match the color of the pubic hair to the particular actor or actress. It's a concept I thought of coming down in the car. Brilliant, isn't it?"

If the Martini was soporific the revue was even more so. Sophomoric and soporific, like wordless naked Shakespeare without the desperately needed poison to put an end to the whole show.

"What are you going to say about it?" Bettina wanted to know, leading him back to the car.

"It's definitely a new concept, a kind of nudist camp version of a Mickey Rooney movie where he shouts, 'Let's put on a show.'"

"That's not the kind of thing I want," said Bettina, frowning. "What's the matter with you, Bering-Strait, don't naked bodies turn you on? Aren't you normal? I expected to finally get a little action out of you. Didn't the naked bums of those actresses turn you on?" In the limo she grabbed his crotch. "Isn't anything going on down there? Here, feel this," and she put his hand on her breast. "What about that, hah? I get more erection out of my nipples than you do out of your willy. Doesn't that dickey-bird ever spread his wings?"

"I don't have flat feet," Serge said, inspired.

"What are you talking about?"

"Prepare yourself for a new concept," he said, pulling his hand away, "the shrink at the Induction Center said I was gay."

"Gay? A Nancy boy?"

"Gay!"

"You're not!"

"I am!"

"Well, Sir Gay, Lord Doily Carte," she said, lighting a Virginia Slim, "no wonder I can't do anything with you. Why didn't you tell me that before? Here I was thinking

54

that I was unattractive to you. How could you let me think such a thing? Everybody wants to get into *my* knickers."

"And I would too, if it weren't for the fact that I'm gay."

"Well, now I understand—and I needn't be hurt, need I? Sex and the Single Girl, and all that."

"Not at all," said Serge. "It has nothing to do with you."

"But didn't I see you eyeing Amanda Quaint at the Lunar Society shindig?"

Serge saw that he must be very careful here. What's a sycophant to do? Of course he realized that he was betraying everything Resurgius stood for, but he had already been certified not only gay, but a coward by the government. Why not make use of it? He could still feel the psychiatrist's stamp upon his forehead. "You saw an exchange of—ideas—of concepts."

"Concepts! Of course! You were having an exchange of concepts."

"You hit the nail on the head, Bettina."

"Don't I always, Bering-Strait. I've got big hair up here and I've got big hair down there, and everybody knows it."

"You said it."

"Of course I did, and I'll say it again."

Serge had been looking straight ahead; now he peeked sideways so that he could see what he knew he would see, the Virginia Slim rowing the air as Bettina Battle repeated, "I've got big hair up here and I've got big hair down there. Now, did you match up the pubic hair with the actors?"

"You bet I did," he said. "I wouldn't let a concept like that pass me by."

"You gay guys are so good at such things, so sensitive," Bettina said, satisfied as a cat who has just ingested a goldfish. Something was going on in the cartoon balloon above Bettina Battle's head, an inspiration, a change of plans. She told the driver, "Take us to Studio 69."

Even Serge had heard of Studio 69. It was famous for famous people, for drugs, Roman orgies, and costumed lunacy. It was reported that the psychedelic lighting—swooping, parti-colored Strobes—and ear-splitting decibels were enough to make one drunk as a dancing bear. People who hadn't had a drink or taken a drug staggered out of the place to their limos.

"My sweet little Sir Gay, I forgive you for your cold-ness, now that I know you're gay," said Bettina Battle, "and I'm going to take you to a place I know you'll enjoy."

"But I have to go home and work on that article about the UNIVAC machines, and I'm already exhausted. I had to get up very early this morning to be at the Induction Center at five-thirty. I shouldn't even have gone to the play to-night. You're running me ragged."

"Nonsense! You're only a snot-nosed kid. Look at me. I'm thirty . . . I'm almost thirty. Besides, I can get you something at Studio 69 that'll keep you awake all night and all day tomorrow, too, better than a rubber thumb up your arse—if you thought that was exciting. How do you think I do it? Where do you think I get my energy?"

"Red diablos?"

"You mean those little candy coated Benzedrine pills? Kid stuff, Bering-Strait! I'm talking about speed or coke. How do you think I keep my figure? I haven't eaten since Whitsun."

"What's Whitsun?"

"It's fifty days before the Late Spring Bank Holiday."

"I thought it was religious—something to do with Easter."

"Not any more. It's a new concept."

She told the driver to let them out at the entrance to Studio 69 and drive around the block until they reappeared. She stepped to the front of a queue that vanished in the perspective of the street lights. A zoo of angry voices jeered them as they were allowed immediate entrance. Bettina had juice.

Temporal aliasing was immediate. The flashing, parti-colored Strobes made Serge's stomach feel like a backward-moving wagon wheel in a classic Western. In addition, the concussive, gut-punching music made his heart flutter. He could see—then he couldn't—then he could. When he could see, it was like seeing stars, exploding stars, exploding in an aurora borealis of colors, and ink-black night befell his every other augenblick. It was hallucinatory. Bettina said, "Isn't this heavenly?"

Serge thought it was like being in hell. "It's the pits!" he said.

"Yes," Bettina cried over the musical blast, "it is wonderful."

The ability to hear came and went like the ability to see. She dragged him through the crowd. Familiar faces, famous faces, appeared suddenly before him, then vanished in the ubiquitous chaos of the place. He saw a former First Lady, a movie star, a Wheaties-box athlete, a famously gay writer, and the great, high-cutting unisex designer, Hevon-she. Everyone seemed to be squirming, like worms dancing on their tails, like snakes in their mating ritual. Some wore masks, some wore capes, some were stark naked, and some looked like they were nine days in the pot. Mysterious hands grabbed at parts of his body. Naughty parts and imi-tation naughty parts, hot and cold, seemed afloat in the air; if you could call the alien-smelling atmosphere, which, if it had a color, would be dark green, air. Serge realized, now, that he was staggering, falling into people, distastefully

57

touching naked flesh and apologizing for it, while at the same time realizing that in Studio 69 no apology was necessary. That's what they were all here for, grab-ass.

In a flash, he saw Bettina, completely naked, handing him a shimmering drink of God-knew-what. "Find yourself a boyfriend," she cried, "you little fairy. This place isn't called Studio 69 for nothing."

And, in another flash, she was gone. But he had spotted something interesting, something recognizable, something that seemed to be alone in a distant corner. With strenuous effort, he achieved the distance between himself and the object of his interest. After all, he told himself, I am a journalist. Curiosity is my bag. He got up close and tried to see what he had seen from a distance. The strobes made it difficult, so he found their rhythm and tried to blink along with them, putting together an image in time, a monument.

Yes, it was he—it! What he had read referred to once as "the white mole of Studio 69." The famous artist of multiple images, the former First Lady back there in the crowd being one of them. Yes, there was the old crazy white mop on top, wild and dry as if it had been hung over a clothesline in the sun. It stared out from behind not dark but black glasses. Could it see or did it care to see? Did it need to see? The white mole of Studio 69 sat at a table on a raised platform, so Serge thought that it must be looking out at the crowd. Serge climbed the steps to the platform and stood behind it. Nobody seemed to notice or to care. Oh, said Serge to himself, this is too good to be true. The white mole of Studio 69 was eating from a bowl of Campbell's Alphabet Soup. Serge leaned down and put his mouth close to the white mop and said, "Why Campbell's soup?"

The artist's head did not turn. The artist showed no surprise. The artist seemed scarcely alive. But a soft voice came in answer to Serge's question:

58

"Because it's cheap. Now buzz off."

Someone took Serge's arm and led him down from the platform. He looked back to catch another glimpse of the famous artist, but, as in a magic trick, the artist had vanished.

Advised by glaze-eyed guides, Serge went hunting for Bettina through the labyrinthine upper regions of Studio 69. He listened for her British accent as he walked dark halls and light and peeked into large rooms and small. The sweet burning, woody smell of marijuana permeated the air and gave him a giggling contact high, lending to the unreality of the hallways. Other odors assailed his nostrils, animal and chemical, and every light in the place, even the merest hallway bulb, blinked on and off in a heartbeat rhythm, causing his eyes to roll in his head and cross behind his spectacles.

Finally, he found Bettina Battle engaged in a very peculiar activity with a man with devil's horns and a woman with a swishing, camelopard's tail. He waited, half blinded, half drugged, respectfully outside the door, until Bettina's final scream suggested satiation, then stepped in and told her that, if he were to write tonight, he must leave, must go home and go to work, as he was already thoroughly exhausted. How much of what he said registered with her, he couldn't tell—the lights, the darknesses, the concussive music, the man with the horns and the woman with the tail, who knew if his words reached what was left of Bettina's mind? But apparently she had heard something of what he'd said, or understood his body language; and somehow got the message. She gave him a packet of white powder, a silver straw, and told him to snort it up his nose, "Make five lines of it and snort it up your nose," she said.

"You'll be able to work all night and feel fresh in the morning. Time it," she yelled, above the ear-splitting boombox of the place. "Spread it out." And she waved him away, returning the valves of her attention to the horny-headed man and the tail-snapping woman. He pushed the package back at her and she finally received it, shaking her head in disgust at him, but the lights flashed out, and he could not see what happened next.

Outside, cabs, as well as dark limos, patrolled the real world.

At home, Old Glory flew upside down at the top of the mast, figuratively speaking, because they had beaten the draft and raised hell at the Induction Center. There was the sense of a crowd forming for a triumphal march. Government had been bested and, in Serge's case, humiliated. Dagmar Bering-Strait was, for once, not furious; she was, in fact, ecstatic; but she had been furious earlier in the day, as she hastened to tell Serge.

"I tried to bite a cop's ear off, but all I got was a mouthful of blue fuzz from his uniform. Disgusting stuff with the distinct flavor of authority."

Auntie Hoover said, "She had to rinse her mouth out and I still had to pick pieces of government shoddy from her tongue. They were going to charge her with assault—"

"I was furious!"

"—when it was clearly we who were assaulted."

"Don't you ladies want to know how Serge got away?" asked Juanna Donna. "You did what I told you to do, didn't you, niño? You came on strong and feminine like Juanna Donna herself would have done."

"Arms akimbo," said Serge.

"And they just let you go?" asked his mother.

"No fuss—they just let me go. They didn't want me. Gays are undesirables in this man's army."

"We're all so proud of you," said Auntie Hoover.

The three aunties of Boadicea Press applauded.

After a ceremonial burning of his draft card, Juanna Donna led an exhausted Serge up to his bedroom.

"I'm pooped," said Serge, and threw himself on his cot in a short Moog heave of compressing springs. "Thank God tomorrow's Saturday and I can sleep late!" he said.

"Juanna Donna has thought you would be like this, but now is time for work. You don't use it, you loose it! You got to get this story out of your system, or you will be one miserable niño tomorrow. I know you. Now get up and hit those keys. I give you a few diablos to get you going."

As she spoke, Juanna Donna busied herself. She sat Serge up on the edge of his cot, rolled his Olympia over his knees, and pushed several pillows behind his back.

"I can't, Juanna Donna dear, I'm exhausted. Give me a break." But he didn't want to disappoint her hopes and said, a little weakly, "All right. Get me some coffee and get me some of those little red diablos. Wake me up! Get me going! It's wonderful to have such a great coach who always has my best interest at heart. You are my true mama-papa. Nobody else cares if I fulfill my destiny."

Juanna Donna dumped a pitcher of ice water on his head. "You make me promise, remember?"

"Did you have to do that? I wasn't asleep!"

"No, but you was trying. Now go get in cold shower and come back and start again."

After a shower and two red diablos, not only did he feel as though he had had a night's sleep, but he felt as if he had more energy than anyone in the world. He felt like Resurgius himself. He could feel the little debilitated straps of his muscles swelling and rippling. Another diablo and he felt mighty, more powerful than a locomotive, faster than a speeding bullet, able to leap tall buildings at a single bound.

"Up, up and away," he cried, sitting down. Wow! He was ready! He had so much to say! A veritable logorrhea was welling up in him, like a pleasant and bottomless regurgitation.

"I feel . . . like Resurgius himself," he cried. "This must be the way he feels all the time. Like a dynamo! I can do it, Juanna Donna!"

"Of course you can, Mighty Mouse. Now hit those keys!" cried Juanna Donna. "Start the next part—go, go, go!"

Pecked raw from before he was a fledgling, and plucked many times thereafter, Serge still had the strength of a raptor whose talons, and even beak, ripped, rat-a-tat, at the torn keys of his Olympia. Oh, he spread his wings wide and soared like a condor over the high Andes of his mind, his telescopic vision seeking out, through his blurred horn-rims, any quiver of the Zorro of justice. In short, his new chapters, imminent and beyond, would even the score.

5

Serge had been up since three the previous morning. The Induction Center seemed like a nightmare from his youth of decades ago, his day at the office a long twilight sleep, "Oh! Calcutta!" was a crazy dream, Studio 69 a walk through hell to get to heaven, his sexual struggle with Bettina Battle—oh my God, he hadn't really married her, had he?—no, that was another part of this multiple act play in which he was starring as a split personality—and his all night wrestling match with his novel—what part of what was that? His head plunked against the Olympia, and Juanna Donna Lorca, like the ministering angel that she was,

She could have been a model, but preferred being a writer. She loved writing and writers and, for her, the best writers were poets. And here she had one buzzing at her door!

He was unprepossessing, a small young man with a baby face and pale red hair, but it was not his physical attributes that interested her. It was the soul of a poet inside of him that drew her to him. She took his wrinkled London Fog and seated him on her couch.

"I'm so sorry just to pop in on you like this," he said. "Lady Be Good" was playing in the background somewhere, Sinatra imploring.

> *Oh sweet and lovely,*
> *Lady be good,*
> *Oh lady be good to me.*

"It's hard to explain," said Serge. "I dreamed about you all night and when I woke up, I had an uncontrollable desire to let you see the manuscript; even though I haven't finished it. I know I told you I'd show it to you when it was done, but I couldn't wait. I had to know what you'd think of it. Maybe you can give me some advice about the ending."

He pushed the envelope containing the manuscript into her hands. "There's a character in it that I think was subconsciously inspired by you—a very beautiful, a very wonderful girl, I assure you—and I was up all night writing about her, and I slept all day, and dreamt about you, and, when I woke up, I felt that I just had to see you. I was on the subway before I knew what was happening. Then I realized that I should call you . . . and why would I think a person like you would be home and free on a Saturday night? I don't know what I was thinking!"

"*A person like me*—what kind of person do you think I am?" She put a silver ice bucket with a bottle of Dom Pêrignon in it on the coffee table, two stemmed glasses, and said, "Will you do the honors? Exactly six and a half twists will do the trick."

"I know," said Serge, struggling to open the bottle, "I watch the French Chef, too."

"Of course you do," said Amanda, tousling his hair. "I love curly hair. You look just the way a poet should look." Amanda Quaint lit a long cigarette and watched as Serge popped the cork and poured them each a glass of Champagne.

"To your story," she toasted. "I can't tell you how delighted I am to see you," she said, fairly bubbling.

> *I am so awf'lly misunderstood,*
> *So lady be good, to me.*

"Do you like 'Lady Be Good'? I thought you would. It's one of those *kinder songs of long ago* that you write about in 'O Popular Moon!'."

"I sort of . . ." he began, hesitantly—"at the party at Hettie Freed's, the first time we met, I . . . I felt, instinctively, you might say, that you were different . . ."

"Different?" She held her glass at eye-level and gave him a quizzical look.

"I know you're one of them—"

"One of what?" She was frowning now, a slight darkening.

"Well, you have to be . . ."

"Be what?" There was a touch of annoyance in her voice this time.

"Well," he said, "you're a writer, an editor. You have to be . . . aggressive!"

> *Oh, please have some pity.*
> *I'm all alone in this big city.*

"As a modern woman, I have to be . . . assertive. But that doesn't mean that every fiber in me isn't female."

"Bettina Battle is female," he blurted, "but you're not like her."

"She's a horrid woman," said Amanda Quaint. "This book you're writing—is Bettina Battle in it? I mean, a character based on her? It's about time somebody did a job on that virago!"

"Well—it's sort of inspired by Plutarch's *Parallel Lives*. It's also sort of a science fiction story, I suppose. Sort of a combination of both. In my life, you see, genres and genders are all mixed up."

"What did you say it was called?"

"Resurgius. I made that up to sound Latin. He's the hero. He's sort of me with muscles."

"You wouldn't be the same with muscles. I'm not attracted to muscle men. I'm attracted to soulful men. Am I really in it?"

"You're the heroine."

"Really! I'm so honored."

"At the end, you and Resurgius get married and live happily ever after. At least, I think that's the way it's going to end. That's the way I'd like it to end."

"I think I'd like it to end that way, too."

The envelope containing *Resurgius* sat on the coffee table.

"Now let me read what you've written so far," she said, assuming an editorial air. "I'm going to take it to my room. You wait here. I'll be back in no time. Play some records. Drink some more Champagne." And off she went, envelope in hand.

In her room, she threw herself on the bed, and began to read.

CHAPTER ONE
THE UPRISING OF THE DONGS

Miz Mandalay, a magnificent Amazon in her early twenties with splendidly developed anti-sex objects, held a dominatrix degree from the University of Xantippe, where she had written an eyebrow-raising thesis in which she had attempted to show that certain ancient Dongs, despite their sexual swinishness, had manifested indications of emerging mental capacity, and had even been capable—this is what had shocked the Univacual Council—of a kind of tenderness. Her thesis was later published on Say-screen. Had the times not become more liberal, this thesis might have consigned Miz Mandalay to the lower levels of government.

But these were turbulent times. Dongs were cracking the information barrier, seeking a newer world, protesting the mandate of Shame-school, speaking boldly out from their hiding places, demanding Dong suffrage and all sorts of outrageous rights. Perhaps the most threatening of these revolutionary Dongs was a Spartacus-like character called Resurgius, known for his Tarzan-like physique, poetic speech, and flirtatious nature. Lately, he had been in the news several times for acts of rebellion that had landed him in Remedial Shame-school, and no one knew what new outrage this caped crusader with the big R shield on his powerful pectorals would commit next.

Whereas, after the Great Succession, Dongs were content to be allowed to walk in the gutters, with their heads hanging, and manifesting upon demand every sign of shame, from reddening cheeks to the squeezing of the legs together, today some dared to go about right on the sidewalks. Some even mingled with the Mize—one infamous Dong reportedly was having a lap-dog affair with a superdoopermodelmiz. This, despite the fact that Dongs were not generally allowed to get close enough to Mize to play at lap-doggie, with their tails wagging.

Of late, small, radical groups of Dongs had been making open protest; as has been said, some had gone so far as to ask for suffrage! (Not that the vote meant anything, even to the Mize; but the idea!)

To liberals of Miz Mandalay's persuasion, these indications of unrest among the once shamefaced Dong population were healthy signs, showing that today's was a healthy, vital society. Some radicals, like Miz Mandalay herself, would give the Dongs a half-vote. She, being a Univacual Council member, knew that the vote was merely symbolic, but also knew that that was precisely what made it important. She would liken it to a valve from which to release the steam of frustration from the pressure-cooker of society.

"After all," she told herself, "the Dongs are human beings, even if they are—well, *Dongs. "*

Ah," sighed Amanda, her heart filled with compassion, and read on. And Serge sat on in terror, waiting, waiting, taking tiny sips of Champagne to wet his dry lips, replaying, over and over, "Lady be Good."

Oh sweet and lovely lady be good . . .
And then Amanda appeared. Her eyes were happy-damp and shined in the soft light of the room. Now she wore a pink negligee that Serge could almost see through to a body that rivaled, if not exceeded, the body of his own literary dream-girl Miz Mandalay. He gulped.

"It's wonderful," she said softly.

"Wonderful? What's wonderful?" Serge said, transfixed.

"*Resurgius*! Your novel," she said with emphasis, seeing that his mind was absent. "I mean, as far as you've gone with it. I really want to know where it's going to go next. Will Resurgius and Miz Mandalay get together?"

Serge had risen to his feet at her entrance. Now she pulled him down beside her on the couch. She put her hand on his neck and felt his fear in the throb of the vein there. Experience told her that he was a virgin and must be treated gently. After all, he was a poet and extremely sensitive. It would be so easy to hurt him and she wanted him so badly now. She must gently, ever so gently, absorb him.

Amanda Quaint leaned over to Serge, framing her face for a kiss. "Well?" she said, widening her violet eyes, and he kissed her, right on her soft red lips. She moved a few inches back, keeping her eyes fixed on his. Her hand was in his lap. "What's that?" she asked.

"Resurgius," he said, flushing.

> *I tell you I'm just a lonesome*
> *babe in the wood,*
> *So lady be good . . . to me . . .*

She drew him to herself and—absorbed him.

In all his twenty-three years nothing so miraculous had ever happened to him. He felt himself enveloped by love, while little estrogens, like microscopic lady-bugs leaping from her, tickled his palm, his chest, his thighs, in a way he might have described in *Resurgius* as heavenly. Oh, oh, oh, this was love. Amanda would have agreed. At last she possessed her beautiful poet, body and soul.

Later, they took a walk on the Esplanade. It was a lovely cool September evening, and many mildly bundled lovers strolled along with them, casting their eyes across the water at Manhattan's blaze of light. They stopped and stared across the harbor, true lovers now, and Serge could not resist reciting a poem he had written at another time when he stood on the Esplanade and looked across the harbor, but that time at the morning lights of Manhattan going dark, a time when he had stood, alone and loveless, and dreamed of having a companion like Amanda beside him to recite it to—

"Across the bay, where East and Hudson meet,
Manhattan forms Prometheus from themes
of stone and steel. I walk the Esplanade
and watch the morning remnant of the moon
pale overhead, slow-swinging scimitar!

I've walked all night, anticipating light.
But more than having light, I want to be
one for whom light adventures into change
and gives me place to say in certain praise
—O light, allow me several such days!"

"Oh, yes, 'From Brooklyn Heights One Morning!' I read it. It's in *The Last Romantic*. Naturally, I just loved it! I've gone out many times in the morning to see the lights of Manhattan go out like that from here, but, naturally, I could never write it like that. It's just wonderful!"

Serge turned to Amanda. "Are you my girl now?"

She studied his magnified, intensified eyes through his spectacles. "Serge, I am. I love you."

"I love you too, Amanda."

Amanda's face grew serious. "I've been wanting to tell you all evening—tell you something—and I'm not sure how you're going to like it. I hope it won't make you angry or hurt or anything . . ."

"Nothing you could ever say would make me angry or hurt or anything."

"Well, here goes . . . you may have heard . . . I'm going to be your new boss. Bettina called me this morning to tell me to come in Monday prepared to take charge. She said

73

you were too inexperienced, and told me quite frankly that she didn't want me either but was overruled upstairs. She's lost her influence with the board." She studied Serge. "You won't mind having me for a boss, will you? Of course, that's only at work, you know. Away from work, you shall be Resurgius. I'll see to that."

"I'd heard you were going to be the new editor of *Women's Omnibus.*"

"Bettina Battle is no more. I start Monday. I know you were hoping for the job."

"Bettina's been teasing me with it. But, to tell you the truth, I'm relieved to know that I don't have to give my all for the cause. I could never see myself as the editor of a magazine anyway. As you say, I'm a poet. But maybe I can be of help to you on the job."

"I know you'll be a big help to me, at first; but, eventually, I'm going to let you write whatever and whenever you feel like writing. You have the soul of a poet and you should do nothing all day but write poetry, and I'll see to it that your little cubicle is undisturbed by mundane matters like food-on-a-stick or UNIVAC III or whatever. You're going to transcend, or I'll know the reason why. I don't even want you to know how I wrested the job from Bettina. Such lovely little ears as yours should be spared the details of the blood sport that is magazine editing. Suffice it to say, blackmail was involved."

"Blackmail?"

"A tape of Bettina being naughty reached the board, I have no idea how."

"Where's Bettina going?"

"She's going to fail upward into politics."

"Oh, thank you, my Jumbly Girl!"

Amanda took his arm and snuggled close, leaned down and kissed the top of his curly head. "My Jumbly Boy," she cooed.

She walked him to the subway, for he had to get home so that he could get up the next morning, Sunday, and work on *Resurgius*. He felt that he was nearing the end, but who knew?

6

Champagne always made Serge hungry and now he discovered that lovemaking with a real woman had the same effect. He was famished, but it was after nine and he didn't want to bother Juanna Donna with his needs. He knew that he need only mention his hunger and Juanna Donna would go to the kitchen and prepare him a hot meal. It would be selfish of him to allow her to do it. So he decided to stop at Schlock's Delicatessen and pick up a chicken salad sandwich and a container of chocolate milk—he was fearless now when it came to chocolate-induced acne; for, after tonight, he must think of himself as a veritable Resurgius, impervious to the minor threats of life. He could almost feel himself turning into bronze.

Now, Schlock's bag in hand, he crossed the street toward Rocky's Rendezvous, peeked in, and saw something shocking. Juanna Donna sat at the bar near the window, in plain view. He had almost passed Rocky's Rendezvous when he realized what he had seen. But Juanna Donna, with a bandage on her nose and a cigar in her mouth, and a bottle of cerveza on the bar before her—she would drink nothing from a bottle, only an appropriate glass—it was impossible!

He took several backward steps to get a second look. What could have happened to her nose that she would need

75

a bandage of such dimensions? She had had only a tiny red spot on her nose, hardly anything at all. Had it become infected? Had she needed the emergency ward at St. Vincent's? Smoking a cigar? Impossible! He entered the bar and stepped up to—*Hector!*

"Hector! What happened to your nose? Why are you wearing women's clothes? Why on earth do you look just like Juanna Donna?"

Hector put a finger to his lips. "Ssshhh," he shushed. "I can get arrested for dressing like this. Sit down and I'll tell you about it."

Serge listened as Hector explained the situation. He told Serge that he had had a nose job with the money Serge had given him. Yes, he knew that Serge meant for him to pay his debt to the loan sharks with that money, but it was not enough, as he soon discovered when he tried to pay an intermediary. The interest rate was so high that he would never be able to pay his debt, over Ten Thousand and going up by the minute. He said he decided that the only thing to do was to become another person—to become Juanna Donna. Well, not really Juanna Donna.

"My new name is Lola Fabiola. The plastic surgeon showed me noses and told me that the one that was best for me was one that looked just like Juanna Donna's because I had the same nose to start with that she had before her operation. What could I do? Then I thought to myself that I should go ahead and make a complete transformation. And here I am, Lola Fabiola, twin sister of Juanna Donna Lorca. We are twins again, thanks to you. And I am safe from the loan sharks. But now I need a job. I can't go back to driving a carriage through Central Park. Not like this. I was thinking of becoming a housekeeper like Juanna Donna. What do you think?"

"I don't know. Wow! You look just like her—except for the cigar. She'd never smoke a cigar, or drink beer out of a bottle. She's too much of a lady."

"Bartender," called Hector Lola Fabiola Lorca, "bring me a glass."

From up the street came the caterwaul of Schlock's untamable burglar alarm, and in the door came a raiding party of badge-waving policemen. In seconds, Serge was lined up with the others along the bar and searched. Fortunately, he had his wallet and identification on him and so was told to leave and warned not to come back to Rocky's Rendezvous. He waited outside to see what became of Hector, a.k.a. Lola Fabiola. Stealthily, the police brought a Black Maria to bear on Rocky's Rendezvous, and, in a few minutes, a half-stripped Lola was being put aboard.

"Get in there, you fag!" cried a cop, and pushed poor Lola roughly through the iron doors.

"What have I ever done to you?" he, she, cried. "Some day we'll fight back," yelled Hector, finally coming out of his closet, becoming the true twin of his sister once again. It was hormone time for Hector—for Lola Fabiola, proud sister of Juanna Donna Lorca.

As the Black Maria pulled away with its sad load of gay citizens, Serge could think of nothing more effective to do than to throw his bag with its chicken salad sandwich and chocolate milk at the retreating vehicle. What would my Resurgius have done, he wondered. Suppose those poor prisoners of love in the Black Maria had been Resurgius' fellow sufferers? How would the great Resurgius have saved them? Serge felt his bronze melting back into weak flesh. He must run and tell Juanna Donna what had happened. She would know what to do. Serge sneaked into the house and crept up to Juanna Donna's room.

Amazed as she was at the story of Hector's transformation and arrest, which Serge blurted every which way he could, like a child telling his mother about his encounter with bullies, Juanna Donna had the presence of mind to call a lawyer.

"Your Auntie Hoover, she una abogada—whats chew say?—she a shyster! Mouthpiece? A *lawyer*, that's it, but I no like to ask her for to help. She likes to get her big nose into everybody's privates. Anyway, she in politics nowadays. Worse than before! And I don't like to use Mr. William Kuntsler, you family lawyer, because everything gets back to them. I'll call Acey Doocy. He understands this kind of problems."

Serge stood by, filled with concern, as she called Counselor Doocy at home and explained the situation to him. Apparently satisfied, she hung up the phone and said to Serge, "Now you no worry 'bout Hector or 'bout me or anything. Everything be fine. Just no breathe no word of this to your mama or your aunties. What they don't knows won't hurt them. Them bodies too busy already."

She handed Serge his manuscript. "I took this from your room cause your Auntie Hoover searches it tonight. She and your mama were furious when they found the inflatable señorita. They take it, but they wasn't half as mad as they be if they read your book."

"Did you read it?"

"Just enough to see what you been up to, you leetle macho, and I know they would not like it, not one leetle bit."

"Why not? What's it got to do with them?"

"Why, it's all about them. And I got to tell you, you make them look pretty funny."

"It's not about them," said Serge, wide-eyed, puzzled, and Juanna Donna could see that he honestly, truly, hadn't realized what he was writing.

"Sergio, you stupido! Anybody can see that it's about them."

"That's not the way a writer works," Serge objected, haughtily. "Sure, I've used a little bit of them, I guess, but each and every character in the story is an amalgam of many people I've met and known over the years."

"Now Serge, how many pipples have you met and know? Except for work, you hardly never go nowhere. You hardly ever *been* anywhere. You stay lock up in your room all the time, like that Boy in the Iron Mask. I'm just warn you, Serge, they ain't gonna like how you show them. The only thing you change is that you made them more real than they are! And, my leetle Negrito, they no see themselves like that."

"Really?" Serge hadn't thought that he was writing realistically but more in the manner of science fiction and fantasy. It occurred to him, not without a certain satisfaction, that he might be more of a Balzac than a Bradbury. It occurred to him that he might be possessed of a strange genius for realism, one of which he was heretofore unaware. A new gravitas weighed upon him, like Earth on the shoulders of Atlas at Rockefeller Center.

"It's past your bedtime," said Juanna Donna. "I mean, if you gonna to write tomorrow and finish that story. Remember, it's Sunday all day tomorrow."

After a night's sleep, Serge woke on Sunday morning, a virgin no more, rolled up his pajama sleeves, and began to write what he thought of as, maybe, the penultimate chapter—in any case, he felt that he was near the end of the story—of his great Balzacian novel *Resurgius,* the first, as he now saw it, of at least fifty of its kind. It was said that Honoré de Balzac, greatest of all French novelists, drank a hundred cups of coffee a day. When Juanna Donna came bustling in with a pot of coffee, he told her, "Keep it coming!"

7

Serge put the last period to his chapter called "The Eternal Triangle," sat back in his chair, and was considering his work, when Juanna Donna swooshed in, wearing a polka-dot babushka, her pale blue raincoat, and straw-topped platform shoes that displayed her beautiful crimson-painted toenails, and carrying a wet pink parasol.

"I'm sorry I no keep up with the coffee," she said, breathlessly. "I go to Mass and then I meet Hector and Acey Doocy, the lawyer. I tell you about it later. I know is a bad thing to interrupt you when you write, but they wants you downstairs right now. You mama and the aunties have that box with the inflatable señorita in it and I think they pretty peesed-off 'bout it. Look like they have a family council. Bettina Battle down there, too. You better hurry. Here, put on your robe."

"Is it pouring outside?" asked Serge, still in the last scene of his story with Resurgius and his beautiful Miz Amandalay making love.

"It drizzle out, but pour poison down in livingroom. You go down, you walk into hurricane. Be brave, mi poco bravo!" Serge was so involved with his story that he was having a hard time understanding the reality of the habeas corpus or what was required of him. Juanna Donna got him into his bathrobe and pushed him out the door. "Don't tell them I gave you that bustious inflatable señorita, or this Spanglish housekeeping he-she will never hear the end of it."

80

Pushed out the door, Serge wondered what a "bustious" inflatable señorita was and how he could possibly be involved with one; but, downstairs, he saw, sitting in the middle of the dining room table, the dusty box with Li'l Abner's naked Daisy Mae on it, gleaming, where angry fingers had clawed the heavy dust away, *bustiously*, through unopened cellophane, and remembered it, of course, his heart sinking, his blood-pressure rising, and his poor, henpecked nerves pulsating like Broadway neon.

His mother, Auntie Hoover, Bettina Battle, and Aunties Charlotte, Emily, and Annie, sat at the dining room table and looked up at him as he entered the room as if he were a despicable felon, a disgusting fellow, or maybe they saw him as a mutant—he tried to interpret their gaze. He remembered now that Bettina Battle had become employed as speech writer for his Auntie Hoover in her quest to get Mayor Dimwiddy elected governor; otherwise, he could not account for her presence. Her expression was a bit different from the others, more of a smirk.

"You sent for me?" he asked.

"Don't be too hard on him," said Bettina Battle to Auntie Hoover. "He looks so cute in his little blue robe, like a baby taking his first steps."

"If you please, Bettina," said Auntie Hoover, in the strained, strangling voice of Eleanor Roosevelt, "stay out of this. Now then, as chair, I call this table to order. Is the whole cabinet present? Is the board all here? What is at issue here is the possession of this female-demeaning sex toy. Why was it found in the dark dust-bunnied recesses under your cot? Speak up, Serge!"

"I'M FURIOUS ABOUT THIS!" cried his mother.

His mind only half present—half, back in the brassiere factory hideout of his novel with Resurgius, Serge couldn't help himself: he giggled.

"Do you find this amusing, young man?" asked Auntie Hoover, at first as though from a great distance, but then catching up with reality. Now Serge was here, in the dining room, the box on the table, where he did not wish to be, and no longer snuggling in fiction with Miz Amandalay doing what comes naturally.

"I see nothing whatever a bit amusing about it," cried Auntie Hoover.

The MacGuffin, the dingus, the box, was on the table.

"The Boadicea Press finds nothing amusing about it, either!"

His aunties sounded like the singing group they once had tried to become. Uncanny harmonics! A clangy madrigal!

"It's not a Greek tragedy," said Serge. "I'd forgotten all about it. Somebody gave it to me and I just stuck it back there. I've never touched it. You can see the package is unopened and you can see the dust on it. I should have thrown it away. I just forgot about it."

"I know why you never went near it," piped Bettina Battle, in an allusion to her belief that he was gay.

"I won't have such a filthy thing in my house," said his mother. "I don't know what to do with you. You're too old to be spanked."

"Oh no he's not," objected Auntie Hoover. "I'd take the backside of a hairbrush and welt his skinny ass."

His mother continued berating him. "When are you going to grow up? You're twenty-three years old and still living up in that garret, and doing God-knows-what up there. It's a disgrace!"

"I shudder to think," said Auntie Hoover, "what's going on up there while I sleep in my bed at night. I've suspected you of unspeakable acts. I remember hearing you making strange noises. Do you remember? I banged on your door and told you to stop."

"I was fourteen!"

"But did you ever stop?"

"It's the wrong kind of doll," Bettina said. "It ought to be Li'l Abner, not Daisy Mae."

"Shut up, Bettina!" cried Serge. "Nobody should worry about that doll when Bettina's around."

"What do you mean by that?" snapped Bettina.

"Yes, what do you mean by that?" snapped Auntie Hoover, but Serge's mother put an end to the inquisition by shouting that she was furious, ripping the package open, and shaking the inflatable Daisy Mae out.

"Look at this disgraceful thing!" She held the doll up by its creamy shoulders for all to see and, with a shocking suddenness, the doll inflated, first bustiously, then with an evil hissing sound, its legs lifted to the ceiling, catching the chandelier, and exploding, orgasmically, on a hot, phallic-shaped 60-watter. His mother was left holding an empty, torn rubber skin, and a mop-like blonde wig. Catching her breath, she said, "I want this wicked thing out of my house!"

Bettina Battle screamed with laughter. Auntie Hoover looked at her as if she were missing a cog. The six ink-stained hands of the Boadicea Press were frozen in a defensive position. Auntie Hoover shook her head. "Go to your room, Serge. But you haven't heard the end of this!"

"You aren't the boss of me," Serge said, under his breath, but he ran up to his room in immense relief, even though he knew, tragically, he would never hear the end of it.

Now there was a mad storm outside and long tears of rain streaked Serge's window. "They're all crazy," he told Juanna Donna, who was waiting in his room with a steaming pot of coffee and a box of Danish pastry.

"You no need tell me," said Juanna Donna. "Remember, I work for them before you was born. From the day I come to this house, I lay down the law to them. They run what they want but I run the house. I'm the head honcho, uh honcha, round here. I was only a few years older than you now. But I was out on my own too long already to let them treat me how they treat you. I was a servant, but I was *UNE HOMBRE*. Trouble is, they think you a snotty-nosed kid. They don't get it that you're a leetle big macho man. You got to assert yourself, leetle negrito."

"But I was never out on my own, like you."

"Me and Hector . . . I mean, Lola Fabiola, we been on our own since we was in short pants. We was on the streets, shining shoes. Tough guys. Plenty macho. Nobody could tell one of us from the other. It was neat. The cops didn't know which one to haul in. In those days, we even use each other's names. Hector would be Juan. I'd be Hector sometime. Then I came out of the closet. I became real me, Juanna Donna Lorca. You *know* twins can't be that different, but Hector, he play macho man, make himself chase muchachas, drinking and smoking like Juan Wayne. Walking around in a closet of his own. But truth catches up—how you say, will out—out of the steenking closet, as Alfonso Bedoya have said in 'The Treasure of Sierra Madre.' Caramba! What a man! Dios! What big white teeth!

"I met Lola Fabiola and our gay Mick counselor, Acey Doocy, down at Rocky's Rendezvous after Mass, and when I first see Hector I think I am looking in the mirror. And you're right, he look just like me again. We twins again! He's out of the macho wardrobe, wearing a very smart knockoff Uncle Milty drag gown, a magenta cloche hat with a gold horseshoe pin, turned up for luck, and a feathered boa, despite the trouble he got in last night. Our Mister

Doocy is going to sue the City, Mayor Dimwiddy, and the police department for Rocky's and all the queens was arrested. We got a lot of angry gays down there. I not be surprised if they has a rebellion—a riot even, someday. They'll call it Rocky's Riot, when the queens gives it back to the cops. But, that's all, now. I don't wanna keep you from you writing."

"I don't know if I'm in the mood to write, now—after that brouhaha downstairs. Besides, love has me distracted, too. I'm in love, Juanna Donna."

"I know you are," said Juanna Donna, tears welling in her eyes. "I could tell from the book. It is good thing, to be in love. Tell all about it in your book. Write it all out. Explain it to yourself. I know what it's like. Juanna Donna has been in love over a thousand times. I have exact number in my diary."

She sighed, fluttering her long dark damp lashes. "It's like you say in that poem of yours that's riding up and down in the subways, 'The Naked Truth'— And even love is true. if we should make it so."

"No, no!" cried Serge. "I was wrong. Love isn't willed. It's a happening. I didn't know it then, what they mean by 'falling in love.' You fall. It just happens. I got that other crap from *The World as Will and Representation.* Schopenhauer."

"Ain't he that Kraut philosopher you tell me 'bout? The one whose disgusted mama kick him down the stairs?"

Serge's eyes went dreamy. He said, "No, you can't will love. It just happens. You really do *fall* in love. You don't do it; it happens to you."

"My leetle niño is grow up," said Juanna Donna, looking at him with damp, proud eyes, full of motherly pride.

"But don't you let mama or the aunties see *Resurgius* or they might kick you down the stairs, you leetle Schopen-hooser. You know your mama. She'll be you-know-what!"

"Furious!"

"You better believe it, niño!"

"Does that mean that you don't think Boadicea Press would publish *Resurgius*?"

"Get real, niño! What you think?"

"But, Juanna Donna, I can't believe that they would refuse to publish a first novel by their own flesh and blood. I just can't believe that."

"I no want to discourage you in any way, bebe. Maybe they not hard as I think they is. The important thing, for leetle Master Bering-Strait, is that he finish the book. We'll worry about the other later."

"I've got to believe they'll publish it."

"Of course you do, bebe. Don't worry 'bout that now. C'mon, hit those keys! I'll keep the coffee coming for you—just like—who's that Frog writer you been talking about so much lately?—Balls Sack?

"Bal-Zac," corrected Serge.

"Si. Balls Sack!"

8

At nine o'clock Monday morning, when Serge arrived at his cubicle, he found a memo from Amanda Quaint on his Selectric. The memo was a summons to her office, which had been Bettina Battle's. In fact, he could see through the glass walls of the editor's office that both women were there, Amanda's Ferragamo boots on the editor's desk, Bettina's ice pick heels chopping a circle around Amanda. It was clear, even at a distance, that they were in discord.

Bettina's Virginia Slim was dancing between her lips as she spoke. Amanda's arms were up behind her head in a manner indicating glacial unconcern. Serge knocked at the door. Bettina strode over and pulled it open, her cigarette still fanning the air, making warlike smoke signals.

"What do *you* want, you great sexless little twit?" spat Bettina Battle.

"I sent for him, you abusive bitch, and don't talk to him like that," said Amanda Quaint, one eyebrow lifting like a feather on fire.

"Well," said Bettina Battle, "now that you're here, maybe you can help me talk some sense into this woman. I'm trying to turn over the helm to her, show her what to do and how to do it, and she won't listen to a word I say. She comes in here and puts her boots up on the desk and won't pay any attention to me."

"Oh, Bettina," said Amanda, not unamiably, "put a sock in it. Serge, I just wanted to tell you that I re-read your manuscript and I'm even more impressed. That's the project that I want you to devote yourself to all day today. Got it?"

"What is that?" asked Bettina. "What project? I already gave him his assignment. He's on UNIVAC III."

"This is something else," said Amanda. "Much more important." She put her index and thumb together and threw Serge a wink. "I didn't want you to sit all day wasting your valuable time on worthless nonsense, without telling you again how much I loved what you are working on, and that you should carry on with it today." She gently waved her hand in dismissal. "Off you go," she said. "I hope you'll have something very exciting to show me later."

Serge walked through the bustling office as if on clouds. Vindication was in the air. In his mind, the music of Amanda's voice blocked out the racket of the office machines and prattling voices that he heard on ordinary days, days before Amanda was in charge, days of the "Battle of Britain," the dark days of food-on-a-stick, sky-mirrors, and UNIVAC III. But suddenly those days came rushing back like a mountain flood.

Behind him, the door of the editor's office flew open, giant voices were heard, and Serge and everyone else in the office had their attention called as to a catastrophe.

Amanda Quaint and Bettina Battle struggled in the doorway of the editor's office, Bettina screaming like a banshee and Amanda roaring like a lion. Amanda got Bettina facing out toward what had become an audience, lifted a booted foot, and shoved Bettina out of the office and into the copy pool. Bettina's dangling Virginia Slim dropped to the floor, spreading brimstone cinders. Everyone waited, breathless. What would she do next? Serge's writer's mind, gleeful of disaster, was ashamed to think that this Donnybrook could make a great scene in *Resurgius*. Perhaps he could use it. Oh, the cold heart of the creator!

In high dudgeon for dignity's sake, Bettina looked out over the heads of her audience. Then she stomped on her cigarette, strode to the elevator—somehow, too fast for human eyes to see, she had gathered up her things—and plummeted sixty-nine floors, a fallen magazine goddess. As far as *Woman's Omnibus* was concerned, that was the ignominious end of Bettina Battle.

For Serge, and perhaps for some others, this incident was a joy to see; but he, at least, had probably not seen the end of Bettina. The dark thought occurred to him that she could still make trouble from her new post with Auntie Hoover and the Dimwiddy gubernatorial campaign. But, he told himself, *carpe diem*, seize the day and be happy. Two such gifts as his compliment on *Resurgius* from Amanda and the departure of Bettina do not often occur in one day.

He was thrilled. From now on, when he looked up from his work and saw the glass tower of power of the editor's office, he would know a friend was there, and a friend in a tower of power is a friend indeed! And so he put himself to work for his friend, trying to grasp the next part of *Resurgius*, thinking, unaware, through his lunch hour.

It felt like some kind of delayed reaction shock. He began to twitch all over. He could feel his eyes rolling in his head; the madman, the lover, and the overwrought poet. He seized his Selectric and stamped out—CHAPTER . . .

He couldn't remember what chapter it should be; he typed on—THE BATTLE OF THE SEXES

He felt it! He was going to write prophesy. Yes, and it was inspired by Plutarch's *Parallel Lives* and Xenophon's *Anabasis* (thought of as an advance) and *Katabasis* (thought of as a retreat). The Mize, led by Jaye Edgahoover with Furius at her side, would advance and the Dongs, under the leadership of Resurgius the Great, would make them retreat.

In an earlier chapter, his Auntie Hoover had become Jaye Edgahoover, Boss of the Universe; his mother, Dagmar, had become her second in command, the frightening Furius. He had already written of them as these characters and now, inspired by the office battle between Amanda and Bettina, he saw a greater conflict—and a longer novel. All of this formed in his mind in a flying instant in time, a shooting star.

What he was about to write, what he was writing, this long war, would take up the whole middle of his great novel, *Resurgius*. The novel was going to be a full-third longer than he had originally planned. He was not near the end at all. He was just getting started. Where had his mind been? Of course there had to be the Battle of the Sexes. How not? Onward! Anabasis! Onward to katabasis, the humiliating defeat of Jaye Edgahoover and Furius, and the glorious triumph of Resurgius! He wrote on . . .

The Ovary Office of the Pink House was a-bustle with activity.

When word was brought back to the Emergency Session of the Univacual Council, that Miz Mandalay had been kidnapped by three Dongs disguised as superdupermodelmize, and that she had been taken away in a golden condom-like balloon, resembling a giant wiener, the members of the Council chorus cried for revenge. This was very much to Jaye Edgahoova's taste, and she made good use of all this feline fury.

"Hear me, Mize," she roared, "the Dongs have stolen from amongst us the flower of our regime, the magnificent Miz Mandalay, whom we all know and love. Who knows if right now she is being tortured with Dong love by that musclebound scoundrel Resurgius? First it was our adored Miz Bet who vanished pneumatically down a tube. Now it's Miz Mandalay. Who will be next? This is war! And I declare it right now on the Dongs!"

"Yea! Yea! Yea!" came the waves of approval. Vox populi, vox dei!

"Long live liberty!"

"Crush the Dongs underfoot!"

"Stab them with your stiletto heels!"

"Put their donkey eyes out!"

"Hang them by their willies!"

"Freedom now!"

"Then let us withdraw, at this moment of crisis, my Atalantamize, my beloved Amazonian angels, to contemplate the grave implications of our actions and to make detailed plans of attack."

A crescendo of approval!

90

"It has been your decision," cried Jaye Edgahoova, flushed with success, "I am only your servant." With which she withdrew. The trembling, quaking, expanding Universe was waiting to see what little ole she would do next. Sturm und Drang on the march.

In the Ovary Office, she called for her chief of Shrike Police, one Furius, a flame-haired ex-barmiz from Hoboken, who was notorious for having bitten off the ears of at least twenty Dongs—it was a dastardly lie that she had bitten off anything else or more than she could chew.

"Furius," said Edgahoova, "you are now looking at the absolute Boss of the Universe. The Dongs have played right into my hands. I can wage open war upon them and get rid of Miz Mandalay at the same time. Get me a Pink Dongly. I'm thirsty."

She took out a cigar, a Dongatella, bit off the tip, and began to puff illegally in a no-puffing zone. Authority says yes to itself and no to everyone else.

Other employees went out to lunch or ate at their desks. Visitors came and went, murmuring approval of the new editor as they passed his cubicle. But Serge was heedless of the advancing day until his phone rang and he heard the meek voice of one of his Boadicea aunties on the line— Annie, the one who had always been most sympathetic to Serge but, as he believed, was too afraid of the others to show it.

"Yes, Auntie Annie?"

"Serge, dear, you must come home now, immediately. We're having a family conference about your book."

"What? How did you get my book?"

"Your Auntie Hoover was looking through your room and came upon her name, or a name that was *like* her own, on a page in your wastepaper basket. Then she did a really thorough search in your room to find the manuscript it came from and could not. However, it occurred to her that it might be in Juanna Donna's room, and she searched there, and found it, among Juanna Donna's flounces. This was just after you left for work. We've all been reading it ever since."

"Did you like it? Did you think it was funny? Did you think it was realistic?"

"Well, Serge, dear, I, personally, thought it was rather amusing, but I'm not so sure your mother and your Auntie Hoover share my opinion."

"Juanna Donna told me that they might not like it, but I've always been absolutely confident that you and Boadicea Press would want to publish it. Am I right? Is that what the meeting is about? Do you want me to come all the way home just to tell me that you are going to publish my book? Can't you tell me now?"

"Well, Serge, it's not my place to tell you what's going on here," she said in a retreating voice. "You'll just have to come home. It's *that* important."

"You always said that a good editor could tell a good book by the first sentence, Auntie."

"That's true! I would have thrown *Moby Dick* right in the fire after reading 'Call me Ishmael!' But that's beside the point. Suffice it to say, Serge, you must come home right away." And she clicked off.

High hopes! They're probably throwing me a surprise party, thought Serge. They must have loved *Resurgius*. After all, Amanda did. Now they want to show me their appreciation of my genius. Only one thing concerned him though—now everyone who counted had read his book, but it, as yet, had no ending, no end to its arc, no climax, no de-nouement. And his deep, considering mind had been work-ing out this problem as he went about his quotidian business

92

or slept. But he must get more black on white as another practical writer, like himself, Guy de Maupassant, had put it, and now, with this interruption, this distraction, how was he to finish? The gossamer structure of his novel's ending, so carefully being constructed in his mind, was being blown apart. He felt a soft vibration of his exquisitely sensitive nervous system as he contemplated this problem—so he set it aside and returned to first and happier thoughts.

Yes, so far, so good. He had written a blockbuster. "From high to low, doth dissolution climb," as Wordsworth, another bookworm, had put it.

He pulled on his London Fog and went back to Amanda's office. "They want me to come home," he told her. "I'm pretty sure they'll publish my book."

"How wonderful!" cried Amanda. "You go ahead home, but you've got to be back here for my inauguration party at five. There'll be Champagne and the works. You wouldn't miss that, would you?"

"Not for a million dollars," he said.

"Off you go then."

It was a hat trick, the third, and final, great gift of the day! Boadicea Press was going to publish *Resurgius*. He had always been sure that Juanna Donna was wrong, that his mother and aunties would love *Resurgius,* once they had gotten over any superficial likeness to themselves—that parallel lives thing—and they would see the humor in it, for they were big-hearted people, not so petty as Juanna Donna believed them to be. They were his family, after all, his nearest and dearest. Blood was thicker than ink, or something like that. They would recognize his Balzacian, Bradbury-like genius—how could they fail to?—and Boadicea Press would be his. He could see a lovely hardbound volume with Boadicea's trademark of the great woman warrior herself on the cover and his name and that of his great hero—*Resurgius*. O joy!

Dashed!

Inside the front door stood Juanna Donna's shopping cart, filled to the brim with groceries. Something was amiss.

Serge walked into a battlefield that was in the throes of an earthquake. It was as if several strong women stood face to face at God's Great Judgment Seat. Cripes! His mother was furious, Auntie Hoover was roaring, and Juanna Donna was a whirling Dervish. The Aunties of Boadicea Press cowered in a group hug.

"I have warn you," cried Juanna Donna, stabbing the air like Zorro with the épée of a long magenta fingernail, her twenty elaborate bracelets clinking, "since I come here twenty-five years ago, that if you ever, ever went into my room snooping, I would leave this house. But I never caught you before," and her voice rose an octave, "but you go into my room to find that manuthing, and Juanna Donna, she never will not *not* keep her word when she say something, so she is leaving this house, and you lazy-assed intellectuals can just learn to cook and clean by yourselves like everybody else. Soon you pipples is be up to you ankles in pig shit!"

"You wouldn't leave me," Serge said, horrified, terrified, mystified, a giant tear rolling down each pale cheek. But no one was listening to him.

"Listen here, Juanna Donna," said Auntie Hoover, waving a finger, "I had every right to find out what Serge was writing about me—about all of us. I'm the boss around here."

"*I'm* in charge around here," cried Serge's mother, furiously. "This is *my* house."

"Of course I meant *you*, dear," said Auntie Hoover. "I'm speaking for you."

94

"Listen ups! This here is Juanna Donna speaking, and, when she say something, she mean what she say. Juanna Donna keeps her sacred word. I am leaving this bughouse. I send for my things," and her hand drew dismissal into the air. "Hasta la vista!"

"Where will you go?" said Serge's mother, placatingly.

"I stay with my sister Hector until I get my own place. I going to retire and live like human being instead of prisoner. I have set aside a bundle. Juanna Donna, she no need this aggravation. She only stay for Serge, and now he grown up and got to learn to be un hombre and stand on his own leetle feet. Youse beeches keep him being like a teeny-weenie niño." She showed them how small Serge was by rubbing her thumb and index together.

"I don't like being bullied by a servant. I *never* liked being bullied by a servant!" cried Auntie Hoover. "*I'm* the boss around here!" she added, jabbing a thumb into her chest. Her face was crimson.

"Juanna Donna is always Capitaine of her ship. And Juanna Donna she is not going to lie to you no more. I gotta new ship just waiting for me if I wants to be Capitaine there; a bigger and better ship than this barge!"

The Boadicea aunties were crying. No one in the house could cook. Would they ever eat again?

"You're the cause of all this," said Auntie Hoover turning to Serge. "Go to your room."

"Yes," said Juanna Donna to Serge, "go to your room! I left you something there, something very important to your future. You can reach me at Hector's." Suddenly, she was gone. Suddenly, impossibly, Juanna Donna was gone.

Serge didn't know which way to turn. Now he was stupefied. "What happened?" he implored of the giant in the sky, his hands up.

Serge's mother said, "Juanna Donna came home from shopping and found us reading your novel."

Auntie Annie said, "She knew immediately that Auntie Hoover had found it in her room and blew up. It was awful. I'm sure she doesn't mean it."

"She'll be back with her tail between her legs," growled Auntie Hoover.

"I don't think so," said Auntie Annie, shaking her head in sadness.

"Why is it all my fault?" begged Serge.

"Because you wrote that disgraceful libel called *Resurgius*," cried Auntie Hoover, "hereinafter," she went on legalistically, "to be known as Exhibit A, or the traitorous Resurgius Papers, insulting every member of this family, making us look like idiots or worse."

Serge turned to Auntie Annie. "Does this mean you're not going to publish my book?" He leaned over the table and, with great stealth, gathered up his dog-eared manuscript.

"I told you to go to your room!" cried Auntie Hoover. "We'll talk about that piece of trash later. Publish it? We'll burn it! Go to your room, I said, you over-aged adolescent!"

"You've made us all furious," said his mother. "Go to your room!"

"Better go," said Aunt Annie.

"Better go," chorused Charlotte and Emily.

Dizzy with confusion, Serge climbed the stairs up to the top of the house. He had never felt so alone in his life. He was ostracized, defeated. But then—a warm greeting, a hint of hope. On his cot lay his overnight bag, fully packed, along with his trusty Olympia in its closed case. And there was a note in Juanna Donna's scrawl.

Dear Niño,

I have watch you grow up, but I have watch that these

womans don't let you grow up. I packed your bag. There's everything you need. This is your chance to make a man of yourself. Follow Juanna Donna into the big world. Take these things and go! You never regret. Call me at Hector's.
      All my love and hopes for you,
            Juanna Donna

The roar of argument followed Serge as he left the house, unnoticed, his overnight bag, containing his precious novel, in one hand and his Olympia in the other. He felt just like Thomas Wolfe leaving Asheville. "You can't go home again," he said, sadly quoting the great Tar Heel. He knew now that he had overstayed his welcome by five years. "*De trop, de trop*, wherever I go," he muttered, rags and quotes always at hand. He should have left home when he graduated from NYU, but it had been so easy not to. Perhaps he *was* an emotionally retarded adolescent, as Auntie Hoover had suggested. Perhaps it was time for him to be a real hero, like Resurgius.

The changeover party at *Women's Omnibus* had already begun when he arrived back at the office. There were balloons and streamers, and over the editor's door was a banner that read, THE QUEEN IS DEAD—LONG LIVE THE QUEEN! AMANDA RULES! Out of the crowd, Amanda materialized. "Come with me," she said, leading him back to the privacy of her office.

"I've left home," he said in a quavering voice, following her, unwinding like a spring. "I'm going to the YMCA. My mother and my aunties hated *Resurgius*. They said it was about them—it isn't of course; I just used bits of them, I admit it—and that it made them look ridiculous. Of course, I had no such intention. They have misinterpreted everything. And, for the first time in my life I've come to realize that they have nothing but contempt for me. *And* Juanna Donna has left us. I'm alone in the world and I'm losing the structure of my novel. I can't remember what to do. It's horrible!" Withheld tears puffed his face.

"Life is like a minefield," he said, unoriginally, lugubriously, "you almost make it across and then something blows up." And he dropped his overnight bag and Olympia on the floor of her office, in desperate emphasis.

"There, there," Amanda said, pushing back a cowlick of his rusty hair. "Calm down."

"Oh, Amanda," he cried, "you're so STRONG!"

"Stuff and nonsense!" Amanda told him that she knew all about it. When he asked how, she told him that Juanna Donna had called her, that in fact, she and Juanna Donna had been in communication for some time.

"She waited down at the corner to see if you would leave and called me immediately to tell me that you had. We are both very proud of you. We know that it was a very brave thing on your part to leave that house. Let me say quickly, my darling poet, that *I* was touched by your lovely portrait of me in the book. You made me a bit ditzy at first, but of course, I understand that the story required it, and I find it incomprehensible that your mother and your aunties can't understand the requirements of fiction. The story is perfectly innocent fun."

"But it has its serious side," Serge put in, puffing up a bit.

"But of course! What's important now is that you write the end of it. Juanna Donna and I have a plan. You are going to live with me and Juanna Donna is going to become our housekeeper. She is waiting, even how, at the house. On the front stoop. So don't keep her waiting. Here, take my keys. As Christopher Marlowe wrote, *Come, live with me and be my love and we will all the pleasures prove.*"

"Oh, Amanda," Serge cried, swooningly. "How wonderful!"

"I have to work late tonight," she added, "after the party. The house is huge and empty and I need somebody to clean it up and to take care of us—especially you, and, more especially, until you have fully given birth to *Resurgius*. I know that Juanna Donna always keeps the coffee coming. Now I want you to take a few days off and finish your novel—which I think is hilarious."

"Hilarious? But don't you think it has a lot of . . . mmm, *gravitas*?"

"Oh yes, Sweetheart, at times it's very heavy."

"Auntie Hoover—who, as you no doubt know, my love, is a lawyer—says its libelous."

"Oh, phooey! She's just worried about any impact it might have on Mayor Dimwiddy's gubernatorial campaign. We'll have the legal department check it out. Your Auntie Hoover won't be able to do a thing. Now, off you go!"

"But Auntie Hoover is dangerous. She's a . . . *Desperada*!"

"Nonsense! In fact, I might as well tell you this now: I'm thinking of serializing *Resurgius* as a spoof in *Women's Omnibus* with my article 'Have Some Feminists Gone Too Far?' as a sort of introduction to it. It'll show the world that there's a new editor in charge, one with new ideas, new concepts. How do you like them apples, my darling?"

"AMANDA RULES!" cried Serge.

9

It was almost midnight when Amanda sat down at the kitchen table in her Brooklyn Heights mansion, weary from her long and difficult first day in command of *Women's*

Omnibus, but buoyed and full of hope for the new order of things, the life she would share with Serge and Juanna Donna.

"So, I will be Capitaine of this big casa," said Juanna Donna, serving them tea.

"Yes," said Amanda, "you will be Captain at home and I will be Captain at work. We'll have the third floor fitted out for a complete apartment for you, just as we talked about. I would have had it done already, but of course I couldn't know just when you would make up your mind to put our plan into action and I've been so preoccupied with work. Serge and I will take the second floor. We'll leave the upper floors locked up and we'll all enjoy the parlor floor, where we'll party. You'll cook and keep house. And we'll have the whole place cleaned up, painted, etc., so you can have a fresh start. Of course, I wouldn't expect you to try to fix this big place up by yourself. It's too much. I'll get you some help. I've been very neglectful. Just sat around and let it all go to pot."

"Why you not care? You are reech and important and very beautiful, so why you not care?"

"Why don't I have an active social life? Is that what you mean? I work hard and I don't need men. Most of the men I meet I don't care for. My Sergie, of course, is quite different. He's not a man, he's a poet. I am not afraid to say I love him because I am not afraid of anything."

"I worship you, Amanda," said Serge. "You are the Queen of my heart."

Amanda took Serge's hand across the table, squeezed it, and continued. "It's exactly what I told you," said Amanda, speaking to Juanna Donna, "the other day when we met for lunch. The world is a difficult place and poets lift us above it. I promised myself when I was a little girl, that I would never fall in love with anyone but a poet. Oh,

100

maybe a composer . . . but no, I like poets better. And I think Serge is a great poet."

"Juanna Donna is so very happy that a woman like you know what a good boy and high brow her Serge is."

Pride goeth before a fall, Serge cautioned himself. Listening to the two of them, he was becoming embarrassed. Who would have thought this situation could come to be? Only a few hours ago, his back was to the wall, so to speak. When he had arrived at the office, he had no idea what he was going to do next; and then, quite suddenly, everything changed for the better.

He understood now that these two sitting with him had been like guardian angels all along, watching over him, helping him to do his work, planning this very situation. What wonders they were! But he had to go to the bathroom and he could not sit and listen anymore to himself being celebrated. How could he ever live up to such—he hoped they weren't misplaced—high hopes in him? How all this came to be, he wasn't certain; but it was a miracle, wasn't it? And a further miracle was that the whole ending of *Resurgius* suddenly constructed itself in his mind, like a golden castle appearing out of nowhere. He saw again how he had planned it to go. It was there, and then he entered a tunnel and it was gone and now he had emerged from the tunnel and it was there again. The mind is an enchanted thing, as Marianne Moore, who herself had once lived in Brooklyn Heights, put it, an enchanted and enchanting thing!

Serge got up and went to the bathroom, his ears burning. He lifted the seat and stood over the commode in frustration. He had to go but nothing came. He struggled. He strained. Still, he could not pee standing up. He felt the disconnect between his body and his mind. Finally, he surrendered to necessity, lowered the seat, took down his pants, and sat down, disappointed.

"I know he loves you like a mother," Amanda said to Juanna Donna. "And I know you'll take good care of him when I'm not here. I'm going to be very busy with the magazine, especially here at the beginning. He needs you to watch over him."

"I start right away. I want to get Serge back to work on *Resurgius*. I promise him I see him through and Juanna Donna always keep her promises."

"So do I, Juanna Donna," Amanda said, taking Juanna Donna by the hands in a kind of unspoken vow of close friendship. "I mean, I want him to finish *Resurgius* as much as you do."

"Because, you see, Miss Amanda," Juanna Donna rolled on, "I was glad when Serge start to write this book. The reason is, to me, that I believe from the beginning that this book would be like—how you say?—*therapy*. I no smarty-pants, Miss Amanda, far from it, but I understands pipple, and I believe he explaining how he feel deep down to himself. They not so bad, those women, his mama, his aunties, they're just all about themselves. They never pay any attention to my leetle Serge when he grow up. I see they keep him like a leetle bird in their big red hands and no let him fly. As he grow, they crush his leetle wings. They don't mean to, I don't think. Just—they don't *see* him. And I know that it must be that you *see* him. You know he is a poet—a special person—and a poet is like a bird that must fly."

"Juanna Donna," said Amanda, "you are a true romantic. I think we're going to get along wonderfully."

"My toothsayer told me that we would. She told me what you would be like to leeve with and I even knew what you would look like before we met, from *Resurgius*. I knew you would be beautiful like Meez Amandalay in his book or like Daisy Mae in the box."

"You mean soothsayer, don't you?"

"No, Miss Amanda, I mean *tooth*sayer. She tells fortune by reading your teeth."

"Oh."

Bells were ringing. Serge woke hugging a pillow that a dream told him was Amanda; but she had deserted him and the bed several hours earlier, before light broke. The telephone was ringing. He went into the livingroom to answer it and discovered that Juanna Donna, who had slept on the couch—Amanda had only used one floor of the house as an apartment—was gone as well. He wondered how a cup of coffee would materialize and thought of the kitchen, where it had always seemed to come from. The telephone rang again. He picked it up, but whoever had been there was gone. He called Amanda at work who told him that she had not called him. She was busy.

"Don't answer the phone," she said. "I don't want you distracted from your thoughts on *Resurgius*." She hung up, but it was good to hear her sweet voice.

He went to the kitchen. There was a jar of instant coffee on the table with a note, compliments of Amanda, telling him to boil water, pour it in a cup, and put the coffee in it. Stir it, the note informed him. Apparently, Amanda thoroughly understood his domestic incompetence. Next, he underwent a terrible brain-strain that ultimately resulted in a cup of coffee, took the steaming cup to the windows, which were French doors, and looked out, considering, as he slowly came to full consciousness, what a lonely soul he was.

He went out onto the patio. A breath of autumn, winding between his skin and the inside of his striped pajamas, chilled him and rose goose-bumps. Directly below him was the long back yard, beyond that the Esplanade, beyond the

103

Esplanade the blown and choppy waters of the harbor, where the Hudson and East Rivers met, and beyond that the towering Manhattan skyline. He went back inside, made himself a second cup of coffee, and toured the apartment with coffee in hand, wondering where and when and how he was to finish *Resurgius.*

The phone rang again and he picked it up to hear his Auntie Hoover's voice say, "Serge?"

"Don't call me here. I will not answer." He banged the receiver on its cradle.

Juanna Donna had left him a note on the coffee table in front of the couch. She had gone to Bethune Street to get some of her things, and would shop on the way back. Her trip would take a couple of hours. Back to work tomorrow, Juanna Donna told him in the note. She promised that the first thing she would do would be to set up a place for him to write. He would miss no more than a day away from *Resurgius*. It was nearly noon. Sun and shadows crossed the kitchen floor. The universe, if not himself, was on the move.

The doorbell rang. It rang again. He felt a sense of urgency. The bell was impatient. It rang again. Serge went on a quick search of the bedroom for a bathrobe—oh, if only he had Resurgius' costume with the big blue cape he could wrap around himself—could not find his bathrobe, hurried toward the door in his striped pajamas, and pulled it open a crack. Cool air and bright sun bedazzled him. Autumnal leaves. Then he saw a long red limousine with a mustard colored streak along its top parked in front of the house. The red limo was impressive and he saw it before he saw the man standing in front of him. He saw the man's straw skimmer before he saw the man. The man's clear blue eyes looked straight into his.

"I'm Quaint, the Wiener King. Got any beer?" The man wore a mustard-colored suit, a red hot bow-tie, and tan rattan-like shoes. He was about Serge's height and weight. Those were the only resemblances. He had a pleasant but bulldog-like face and there was a huge, ginger, walrus mustache under his sharp nose. His voice sounded as if he were chewing gravel. He must have been eighty years old.

"I say, are you altogether there, son? I repeat, I'm Quaint, Amanda's granddaddy. I stopped by to see her at the office and she told me to come down and take a look at you. She said she's gonna marry you. This was my house before I gave it to Amanda," he added, pushing Serge aside, establishing his authority, and heading for the kitchen.

Serge followed him, leaving the door wide open behind him. "Here's a box of wieners," said the Wiener King, "Quaint Wieners," and he walked into the kitchen and dumped the box on the kitchen table. "Now how about those beers?"

The Wiener King sat down at the table and looked up at Serge. "Son," he said, "one look at you at the front door and I knew something. I'm Quaint and I'm quick. You've got something missing. What do you suppose it is?"

Serge stood looking at the Wiener King, fully aware now of who he was dealing with, but dumbstruck.

"What you're missing, son, is a mustache! A good thick beaver mustache would make a man of you. Look at me! Everybody does! And they do what I damn well tell 'em to do because I've got a voice like a bear and a mustache like a beaver pelt. You need hair on your face. You're smooth as a boy. Hell, you're as smooth as a girl. But I don't hold that against you. I didn't realize what a gruff voice and a big mustache could do until I was nearly thirty. It was just about then that I went into the wiener business, and the bigger my mustache got, the bigger my wieners got. I drink nothing but beer and eat nothing but wieners. This diet has made me disgustingly rich, and kept me slim and healthy. I'm almost ninety years old, you know," he yelled. "I know that's hard for you to believe. Wieners bring optimism and optimism brings optimal health. Now where's that beer that you keep promising me?"

"I don't know if we have any," Serge finally got out.

"Hellfire and brimstone! How can you live without beer? It's the staff of life in a bottle. Wieners are the staff of life themselves, so beer is like a wiener in a bottle." He gave Serge the once-over. "Why is a young man your age still in his pajamas at this hour of the day? Oh, never mind! Did I tell you, I stopped by to see Amanda at her office and she told me to come down and take a look at you. She wants to marry you. You look O.K. to me. Hell, you must be or she wouldn't want you."

"Marry me?"

"Why, yes, of course! What do you think you're doing here? She told me you're some kind of poet. But that's O.K. You won't need money in this family. She makes a lot and I have the rest. The main thing is that you're a good decent chap. But I still say that that baby face needs some hair on it, poet or not."

There was a racket in the hall and five workmen in paint-splashed coveralls walked into the kitchen. One of them said, "We're the painters. You left the door open so we came in. Where do we go? What do we do?"

"Hello boys, I'm the Wiener King," said the Wiener King. "You boys got any beer? When I was a house painter, which I was when I was young, we always brought beer along with us, and nowadays they got those cooler things to keep it chilled. We didn't have them. We had to drink warm beer. I repeat, boys, where's the beer? If you've got the beer, I've got the wieners, as you can see. Had any lunch?"

In ten minutes, five workmen, Serge, and the Wiener King sat around the table, drinking beer and talking, while the aroma of grilled wieners filled the kitchen, the Wiener King regaling the painters with tales of ancient days when he himself had been a house painter in the Bronx.

"Now let me tell you something REALLY interesting," the old man shouted, clearly feeling his beer; but he was stopped by the cling-clang entrance of Juanna Donna and Lola Fabiola, a.k.a. Hector.

"Now let me tell *you* something really interesting," said Juanna Donna. "This party is over! You painter men get upstairs and get busy. Third floor. You know what to do. And make room for movers. They be bring up my things. Serge, you been drinking beer?"

"No, no, Juanna Donna," said Serge, shaking his head, "only coffee." Serge answered the elaborately costumed person who asked him the question because he assumed that only Juanna Donna would ask such a question; but, in all truth, he wasn't sure whether he was speaking to Juanna Donna or Hector, so alike were the twins now. They had become doppelgängers again.

When he first knew them, as a little boy, they were identical; then Juan turned into Juanna Donna, gradually, but before his eyes, and now Hector had turned into Juanna Donna, or Lola Fabiola, and he could hardly tell them apart but for what they said. After a moment or two of sharp contemplation, Serge stretched out an arm and indicated the person he thought was Juanna Donna.

"Mister Quaint, I would like you to meet our house-keeper, Señorita Juanna Donna Lorca, and her bro—eh, sis-ter—Señorita Lola Fabiola." He scratched his head. Did he get it right?

107

"Manny Quaint here, Amanda's granddaddy," yelled the Wiener King. He got to his feet and gave the twins a courtly bow. "I may wonder how many beers I've had, for I'm seeing double. How amazingly charming it is to meet two such attractive señoritas. Nature might have been satisfied with one. Mother nature might have thought that she had pressed her powers to the limit in creating one such beauty, but *two*—two perfect specimens of womanhood— well, it simply takes my breath away. If I had the stamina that I had in youth—say, at seventy—I wouldn't know which one of you to pursue first. But one question might clear my mind. Which one of you likes wieners?"

"Both of us like wieners," said Juanna Donna, taking two from the table and handing one to Lola Fabiola.

"Alas," cried the Wiener King, "I am confounded. If only I were a polygamist and could marry you both, my Spanish beauties."

"Then we would be very rich?" asked Lola Fabiola.

"You would indeed, ladies," yelled the Wiener King, "but there's a law against what I have in mind, even though with enough beer and wieners aboard, it's a fact that I can run in two directions at once. In other words," he said, "I can defy nature itself," and he winked and donned his skimmer. "Serge," he said, "I feel a bit wobbly. See me to the front door, will you?"

Two of Juanna Donna's movers carrying a heavy chest of drawers toward the staircase passed them in the hall.

At the front door, Serge had the wit to ask, "Do I meet with your approval, sir?"

"Oh, you already had my approval when I came. Whatever Amanda wants—well, Amanda always does the right thing, so I know you're the right thing for her. I just wanted to get a look at you, see what it is that she likes about you, that she loves about you, and I think I can see it.

I think I see a good heart and a sweet nature. Don't hide your light under a bushel, son. If Amanda loves you, you have a right to be proud. There's a durnblasted good reason for that love. But you need some hair on your face. Grow that mustache!" The Wiener King's chauffeur came up the steps and took him by the arm.

Serge hadn't thought so far as parental approval. "Do you think Amanda's parents—"

"Don't worry about Amanda's parents. I'm the one you have to impress. What I say goes. They're rich from having me; I'm rich from having money. I'm the *law. I'M THE WIENER KING!*"

The patient chauffeur helped the Wiener King down to his limo, where the W.K. turned around and yelled, "Later!" And, with one last wave of his skimmer, he was off in his Wienermobile.

The after-image of the Wienermobile had not yet cleared from Serge's mind when Bettina Battle appeared at the foot of the steps as if materialized by a Roddenberry beam. She looked up at Serge. "Who was that?" she called. "Wasn't that the Wiener King?"

"Bettina! What are you doing here?"

"I'm a reluctant emissary from your family. They've had a change of heart. Your Auntie Annie talked to your mother and your mother talked to Auntie Hoover and Auntie Hoover sent me to get you. Why won't you answer the phone? You could have saved me the trip. I had no desire to come down here to Brooklyn. I don't particularly want to see you, after the way you've treated me, and I certainly don't want to run into Amanda. But I am under orders from your Auntie Hoover to bring you home for your mother's sake. She's not furious any more—*au contraire*. Aren't you going to invite me in?"

"All right," said Serge, stepping aside, "if you must; but this is a very busy house today."

A large white van pulled up and parked where the Wienermobile had been. A number of bustling men appeared from its recesses and in seconds were carrying pink bathroom fixtures up the steps, forcing Serge back. Serge heard Juanna Donna directing them up to her apartment. The men brought in a bath and shower unit, a sink, and, following behind the bobbing commode, Bettina Battle entered.

"I've been here before," she said, seizing Serge's hand and pulling him into the kitchen behind her.

The house rang with the hammering of construction, and the workmen who passed through the kitchen did double-takes, seeing Bettina, statuesque and pulchritudinous in her mini-skirt and five-inch heels. Serge saw their eyes pop and knew that their mouths were watering. "Fix me a nice cup of tea," she said, sitting down at the table.

"I get it," said Lola Fabiola through seven veils, innocent of Serge's desire to get Bettina out of the house.

Bettina lit a Virginia Slim and let it dangle from her crimson lips while she talked. "I've been ordered to bring you home," she said, "dead or alive. I just have to get you there and then you can do whatever you want after you've seen them. My job is at stake. Your Auntie Hoover doesn't take no for an answer. I'll lay my cards on the table. How much do you want?"

"Much what?" asked Serge, not getting her drift.

"Money, of course. I'll give you five hundred to come to Bethune Street with me. This is the first important job your Auntie Hoover has given me as her assistant and I've got to get it right. Five hundred bucks isn't bad for a trip to the Village, is it? Look, the money's about two-to-one, so I'll make it five hundred pounds. What do you think?" She

110

took a sip of tea from the cup Lola Fabiola had set before her and blew a tornado of smoke at Serge.

"I wouldn't go back with you if you gave me the Exchequer and threw in Fort Knox. I wouldn't go anywhere with you anyway. I know what you get up to in that damn limousine of yours. And Amanda wouldn't like it either."

"Amanda! Amanda! Do you know what that bitch girlfriend of yours did to me? She blackmailed me! She taped me when she was in my car with me and gave it to the board of directors of *Omnibus*."

"Magazine editing, I've heard, is a blood sport," said Serge. "Amanda told me so."

"Aren't you shocked, Mister Goody Two-Shoes?"

"A woman's got to do what a woman's got to do," said Juanna Donna, appearing in the doorway. Bettina looked at her, whirled about in her chair, and looked at Lola Fabiola.

"My God!" she cried. "There're two of you. I thought the one who got me the tea was Juanna Donna. Who's the other dervish?"

"That is my bro—" started Juanna Donna—"my sister Lola Fabiola. Maybe when you come to Bethune Street you saw my brother Hector. Well, he is my sister, and once again he is my twin. I am glad there are two of us but I am sorry there is even one of you, Mzzzzzz Battle. Why you let her in, Serge?"

"Just one minute here," said Bettina Battle, pulling herself up to face an enemy attack. "Who do you think you're talking to?"

"Juanna Donna know who she is talking to, who is not who she pretend to be. Juanna Donna, she hate a fake, a big tall fake in a mini-skirt." She went around the table and lifted Bettina to her feet, stood her on her towering heels.

"You big bony stack of stink," she cried. "Juanna Donna has dream of giving you heave-ho lots of time from

Bethune Street but now in Amanda's house, I can do it, because I am Capitaine here."

"Unhand me," cried Bettina, "you walking stack of carnival tents!"

"I unhand you O.K., because I no like to touch you, you phony phooey! I catch you stand up to pee at Bethune Street. You are what Serge call a Dong." She looked at Serge and Lola Fabiola and pointed at Bettina.

"This is no woman! This is like me and you, Lola, but too phony to be what she is. She got a string on her crotch that she tuck back up. *He* got a string, the beech!"

Now she lifted Bettina Battle and carried her kicking to the front door, Serge and Lola following. "You go back to Auntie Hoover with your tail between your legs and she take care of the rest of you."

"Serge," cried Bettina, "for God's sake, help me!"

Juanna Donna set her—eh, *him*—down on the stoop and closed the door after her—eh, him. A couplet from Edgar Allan Poe popped into Serge's mind—

Is all that I see or seem
But a dream within a dream?

Serge went to Amanda's bedroom, found his clothes, and got dressed. No one noticed as he left the house. It was good to be out and away from all that hammering and yammering. He spent the afternoon contemplating the sliding slate of the harbor from the Esplanade, watching people promenade, putting the parts of the end of *Resurgius* together in his mind, and watching the sun slide down into the west. And then, not soon enough, it was time for his angel to come home, and he returned to the house. What a relief! The workmen were gone. Hector—Lola Fabiola—had gone back to Bethune Street. Juanna Donna was making *arroz con pollo*. The house was quiet. Later, after dinner, alone, he told Amanda what had happened with Bettina. "How could I have missed such a thing?" he asked Amanda. She saw that he was in a state of consternation.

"So far as I know," said Amanda, "only Juanna Donna and I knew about it. Look at her. No one else could possibly tell." Amanda told him that Bettina Battle was out of their lives forever. She told him that she had talked to Juanna Donna about what had happened, and that he should not concern himself with it, but concentrate his attention on finishing *Resurgius*.

There was no question that Amanda knew best, that she was the Captain of him, so he listened to her advice, dreamily snuggled his head into her more than ample bosom, and went to sleep while watching Resurgius, broadsword in hand, slaying a dragon that looked rather a lot like Auntie Hoover.

Waking, alone again, Serge, sandy-eyed, found his way to the bathroom. He stared at himself in the mirror. He needed a shave. He decided not to touch the area under his nose and above his upper lip. Staring hard at his reflection, he thought he could detect the beginning of a bushy red mustache, something that might one day resemble the Wiener King's. But perhaps it was only morning shadow enhanced by his hopeful imagination. He sat down on the john to pee, realized what he was doing, and jumped up. He turned around and lifted the toilet seat and filled the bowl the way Gargantua had filled the Seine, the way Resurgius had filled the River Slime. O joy! O gratification! *Viva machismo!* Hooray for John Wayne!

"Good day, Pilgrim," he said to his willy, shaking the last drops from it, "and thanks."

Serge found a pot of coffee waiting for him in the kitchen, and a note directing him to the second floor, where everything had been prepared for his task of finishing

Resurgius. He had slept late again, and Juanna Donna had to shop; but she would be right back, her note informed him. Walking about in his P.J.s., Serge began to read his penultimate chapter: "A Byzantine Betrayal."

"O, betrayal!" Resurgius cried, "O, treachery!"

"Alas," said Miz Amandalay, climbing in next to him, "she loved you not too well, but, rather, too wiseguyly."

Wiseguyly! It was as if he had intuited Amanda's knowledge of Bettina's secret. He began to put things together. When Bettina kidnapped—well, commandeered—Amanda from the Lunar Society party, something must have happened. Amanda must have discovered Bettina's secret—and the tape!—she must have recorded everything Bettina said—and he had enough experience with Bettina to imagine what that might have been—and later sent the tape to the board. *Blackmail!* Now he understood clearly. Oh, what a mighty woman was his Amanda Quaint! If only she could share her strength and empower *him*!

Everything had been arranged for him—chair, table, typewriter, and paper. He sat down at his Olympia, and—DA-DOT, DA-DA!—began—CHAPTER . . .

Again, he couldn't remember what chapter it was. He was never any good at numbers.

Losing shame and gaining pride with every advance, the Dongs had fought their way to the Pink House. It was over for the Evil Mize. The rest of the female population sent emissaries to the Dongs to inform them that they, too, were happy to be out from under the oppressive thumbs of the dictatorial Mize. The war was over.

Handy Mandy, as Resurgius sometimes called Miz Mandalay, because she had been so helpful to him during the war, asked Resurgius what he thought should be done now that they were in power.

"The New Order should not be one in which either sex is in a superior position, nor should it be one of equality—male and female are obviously not the same. They are two halves of a whole. In other words, they are complementary." He studied the beautiful woman before him. "Ah, but you are my better half."

He went on: "This revolution business is too much for me," he said, pushing his hornrimmed glasses up through his lush locks to the top of his extra large and scholarly head. "I just wish I could go off to some distant paradise and lead a quiet, meditative life, reading the rest of the Western canon, re-reading all the wisdom books, and studying Eastern philosophy."

You're just tired," Miz Mandalay soothed. "You've been through hell."

"To hell and back," Resurgius said stoically.

"My hero," Miz Mandalay commented, squeezing his powerful thigh.

"Mandalay?"

"Yes, dear?"

"Would you consider giving up all this—the political life, I mean—and running off with me to a desert planet, where it would just be you and me and the drifting meteorites?"

"Well, dear, I do so hate to see you give up all that you've fought so hard for; but, naturally, my love, whither thou goest, I will go. In the face of love, the life of politics seems but pale mundane trash. After all, as Jaye Edgahoova might say, politics is nothing but the profound entertainment of the people. I am no longer that interested in entertaining the people. I am in love, and therefore selfish; and perhaps that is the best way to be. At least, if I'm minding my own *business, I won't be doing them any harm, poor devils. Pity poor people, they have no sense. I often wonder why they do what we tell them to."*

"Because they're afraid to think for themselves. Because they mix us up with their ideals, their hopes and dreams. They're the lemmings and we are the force of the ocean, drawing them to us. That's all."

"It's really quite sad."

"Then you'll go with me?"

"Anywhere, anytime."

"Tomorrow morning, to the moon. From there we can get the shuttle on to Mars."

"It'll be like an old-fashioned honeymoon."

"Let's start tonight. The honeymoon part, I mean."

"Oh, you!"

But it was only a dream, and in dreams begin responsibilities, as the ancient Irish were wont to say. They knew that people, all people, needed them as they represented, as a power couple, the true balancing and partnership of the sexes.

Next day, Resurgius brought charges against Miz Bet and banished her to the dark side of the moon, where rumor had it that she joined Edgahoova.

The disposition of Furius was another matter. The woman was half mad, and so in good conscience could not be punished. Resurgius, after much deliberation with Handy Mandy, decided to have her institutionalized in one of those charming new Neptunese padded cellular houses in Washington Square in Greenwich Village.

Resurgius and Handy Mandy were married. Both died in office, Resurgius first—of a heart attack from carrying Handy Mandy's luggage—and Handy Mandy, in her sleep, twenty years later. Both were beloved by the populace.

10

"That last chapter is wonderful," said Juanna Donna. "I so glad for you that you have done it and so proud of you, my little Mighty Mouse. No, no, Juanna Donna has said wrong. You not my little Mighty Mouse. You my mighty macho man, Resurgius himself! I never call you anything but my mighty macho man again, 'cause look what you have done!"

"And Juanna Donna, I have more big news for you. You know my problem . . . "

"You mean the way you has to go to the bathroom?"

"I do it like John Wayne now. I could stand up and do it right against a tree."

"Is a miracle! And you know what do that to you? Is because you wrote this book. And what is that I see beneath your nose? Don't turn away. You don't fool Juanna Donna. Is a leetle red mustache coming out there? Very macho!"

"And I owe it all to you, Juanna Donna. To Amanda, and to you and those little red diablos that kept me going when I was so exhausted at night."

"Phooey! There is no such thing as little red diablo. I have been giving you Doctor Spinoza's Red Regulators. They for constipation, sluggishness, and change of life—which both of us is going through. See? You stand up at the toilet. They make me sit down. You no think I would give my bambino bad drugs, do you? I would never do that!"

"But why did they work? I mean, how did they keep me up to work?"

"They didn't! Is all a state of mind, niño—I mean, Resurgio—all a state of mind. The coffee must have helped, but mostly it was just being encouraged. Encouragement what inspired you."

"Well," said Amanda, late that evening, as she and Serge sat together in bed, "I love it! But, as your editor, I think you're going to have to re-write that whole last chapter.

"No! What's wrong with it? Juanna Donna said it was wonderful."

"Why just everything! Why should you die and I live twenty years more?"

"That's what the actuarial charts tell us. On the average, women live twenty years longer than men. Besides, Miz Amandalay isn't you and Resurgius isn't me. They are rounded, compound characters, each made from several people."

"Nonsense," said Amanda. "It's plain as day who they are. I don't like Handy Mandy. That's an awful name."

"But remember, in an earlier chapter, Miz Mandalay tells Resurgius to call her that. She says, 'From now on, I want you to call me Handy Mandy. Miz Mandalay is my old Univacual name'."

"And another thing," said Amanda, ignoring him, "all of these names have to be changed. I can identify everybody in this story. And what's more, I want a more romantic ending."

"Are we having our first argument?"

"Now, don't pout, Serge! Say, what's that under your nose? Are you growing a mustache?"

"Well—"

"Don't worry. I like it. It gives you a certain—*savoir faire*." She took off her reading glasses, put them and the manuscript on the bedside table, and slid an arm around his neck. "Come on, Sweetie Pie, come close."

Next morning, Juanna Donna woke them. "I has a message for you," she said, nodding at Serge. "Mama call and wants you come to Bethune Street."

Well, it was here—the moment he had dreaded. He must confront his family and tell them that he was not going to return to them; that he had a new life. But now that *Resurgius* was done, and with his new red mustache on his prow, he felt that he could do it.

On his way to the subway, Serge spotted the Quaint Wiener airship sailing off in the distance over Brooklyn, a red wiener hovering in the blue morning sky. He told himself it was a talisman, that it indicated that his meeting with his mother and his Aunties would not go too badly.

At Bethune Street, the door was opened by—

"Hector!"

"No, no, no, señor Serge! I am proud to be Doña Lola Fabiola Lorca, the true queen of the Lorcas. My sister, Juanna Donna, is only pretender."

"It's amazing," said Serge. "I only just left her and I feel as if I'm seeing her again. It's as if she'd been transported in a time machine."

"Come on in, your mother and your aunties are waiting to see you. Be nice. I think they want to make up with you."

Serge's mother, his Auntie Hoover and the Boadicea triplets were gathered in the living room, as for a family conference. Serge felt as if he had entered a scene from a Victorian novel. Mother and aunties didn't seem to know quite what to say or how to say it.

"It's good to see you all looking well," Serge said. It seemed a bit formal, so he added, "Look, I'm sorry if I caused you any pain. But I'm out on my own now, and I'm going to stay out, and—"

"Oh," said Auntie Hoover, "we don't mind that you've left us . . ."

"No," said his mother, "we're glad to see that you're standing on your own two feet. We never meant to hurt you. After all, you're twenty-three years old and you should be out on your own. My God," she cried, "you've got a whispy whisk-broom under your nose!"

"And maybe," Auntie Hoover rolled on, "we lost track of how old you were because sometimes it seemed as if you were never going to go out on your own. We're not really mad because you left home. But did you have to make such fun of us, ridicule us that way, in that awful book? It was shocking to think that you hated us so much. After all, we're just women, and you were a boy, and maybe we made mistakes bringing you up, but we always loved you."

"We always loved you," echoed his mother.

"We always loved you," chorused the three Boadicea aunties.

"And you made us look like monsters," said Auntie Hoover.

"But the characters in that story weren't *you*," said Serge.

"Jaye Edgahoova?" Auntie Hoover wanted to believe Serge but looked doubtful.

"And anyway," said Serge, "I'm a poet who wrote a novel, not a novelist who writes poetry. I should stick to what I'm—well, I write better poetry than I do fiction."

"I should say," said his mother. "The novel made me furious, and I'm so relieved to hear that you really didn't have us in mind."

"We should say," chorused the three aunties. But Aunt Annie threw him a wink.

120

He couldn't help smiling, and suddenly everybody was smiling, even Lola Fabiola, standing in the doorway with a tray laden with coffee and croissants.

"When can we all meet your Amanda?" asked Auntie Hoover. "Is it true, that she's related to Manny Quaint, the Wiener King?"

"She's his granddaughter."

"I should have Bettina contact him about a campaign contribution," she said. "He's richer than a king."

"And a wonderful old guy," said Serge. "He's going to buy us a slam-bang wedding."

"When's it to be?" asked his mother, full of uncharacteristic, girlish excitement.

"This coming June, of course. Amanda wants to be a June bride."

A comedy—even a sex comedy—thought Serge—should end with a wedding. And in June there was a photograph on the cover of *Women's Omnibus* magazine of the wedding of the Wiener King's granddaughter, Amanda Quaint, and the young poet, Serge Bering-Strait.

The ceremony took place in Central Park, at the Tavern on the Green, where the Quaint Wiener airship had touched down on a day when the sky was blue as only a wedding day sky can be. The photo on the cover of *Women's Omnibus* showed the beautiful bride helping her dashingly mustachioed groom into the gondola of the famous Quaint Wiener airship.

Whatever secret location they sailed off to, the honeymoon would certainly be in paradise. Yes, Amanda had removed the ring from Serge's nose and put it on his finger, and Serge just knew that, like a prince in a fairy tale, a fairy tale with a beautiful princess, they would live happily ever after.

When the Sex War ended
with the slaughter of the Grandmothers . . .
                                —W.H. Auden

RESURGIUS REDUX
The Sex War

by

Serge Bering-Strait

Dedicated

to

Amanda Quaint Bering-Strait

and to

Juanna Donna Lorca,

without whose help, forbearance,

and little Red Diablos,

I could not have written this great work

1

NOTA BENE

Serge Bering-Strait here. I have just finished reading E.M. Schorb's account of my life to date, and am amazed at the degree of intimacy he has achieved in it. It appears that he has been my Doppelgänger, my vademecum—I blush to say it—present even at those sacred intimate moments when I was with my beloved Amanda.

Greenwich Village gossip has it that he is an almost blind bard, who looks out at the world through large horn-rimmed glasses very like mine, very darkly, but perhaps those who say so are having me on, which is N.Y.U. slang for kidding. As Schorb has accurately described them, my mother and aunts, the sum total of the sad family I was born into, are clinicians of emotion, shallow of human feeling, only passionate in their desire to make themselves known to the ochlocracy and to tell it how to live—but certainly not to share the world with it. As for their attitude toward me, the young person in their midst, they take me for a nerdy and pimply adolescent. They ignore my genius-level I.Q. at their peril. Resurgius Redux is my response to their ignorance of the real me.

Vengeance is mine!

S.B.-S. I am Resurgius.

2

THE UPRISING OF THE DONGS

Politics, as the word is commonly
understood, are nothing but corruptions.
—Jonathan Swift

Miz Mandalay, a magnificent Amazon of twenty-five with splendidly developed anti-sex objects, held a Doctorate in Liberal Tyranny from the University of Xantippe, where she had written an eyebrow-raising thesis, later published on Say-screen, in which she had attempted to show that certain ancient Dongs, despite their sexual swinishness, had manifested symptoms of emerging mental capacity, and had even been capable—this is what had shocked the world—of a kind of tenderness.

Had the slum-lord class not become more liberal, that thesis might have consigned Miz Mandalay to the lower levels of governance. But these were turbulent times. It had become possible to say the un-sayable of ten years before. Dongs were cracking the information frontier, seeking a newer world, speaking boldly out from their hiding places, demanding Dong suffrage and other outrageous rights. Perhaps the most threatening of these revolutionary Dongs was a Spartacus-like character called Resurgius, known for his Tarzan-like physique, poetic speech, and flirtatious nature.

Whereas, after the Great Succession, Dongs were content to be allowed to walk in the gutters, with their heads hanging, and manifesting upon demand every sign of shame, from reddening cheeks to the squeezing of the legs together, today they went about right on the sidewalks, and mingled with the Mize (though they were not generally allowed to address them unless spoken to); and of late small, radical groups of Dongs had been making open protest. Some had gone so far as to lift a leg and ask for the vote! (Not that the vote meant anything, even to the Mize; but the *idea*!)

To liberals of Miz Mandalay's persuasion, these indications of unrest among the once shamefaced Dong population were healthy signs, showing that today's was a healthy, vital society. Some, like Miz Mandalay herself, would give the Dongs the vote. She, being an inner council member, knew that the vote was merely symbolic, but she also knew that that was precisely what made it important. She would liken it to a valve from which to release the steam of frustration from the pressure-cooker of society. After all, she told herself, the Dongs *are* human beings, even if they are Dongs.

Miz Jaye Edgahoova, and others of conservative persuasion, felt differently. As Miz Edgahoova, a poco-porcine middle-aged Miz, put it: "These Dong protesters are highly dangerous, potentially. Let us recall that our own Movement started in protest. And let us remember, further, that in the antique days protest did no real good for us. It is not in the nature of power to give itself away. Most of you are too young to remember, but we who date back to the time before the Great Succession, do—that we used to say, *This is a Dong-dominated society*. Of course, what we young vaginal revolutionaries did not understand at the time was how right we were. In those days, what we were naively doing was *asking* Dongs to stop dominating us and to empower us. It never seemed to occur to us that the fact that they *did* dominate indicated that they *could*—indeed, had, always. Why?

Because dominance, after all, *is* power. And you cannot *ask* that the powerful cease being powerful. How can they stop being what they are? No, we came to realize that we couldn't simply ask for power—power is something you have to *take*. If you can take it, you are powerful; and if you can hold it, you remain powerful.

"Now today's liberals, the Dong fellow travellers, are asking us to give and give. Give in on this point, give in on that. Give in, and let the Dongs have the vote. Remember, that was the very first mistake the Dongs themselves made. That was the step that led to the Great Succession. The tactic in those days was to make the Dongs feel ashamed of their strength. We were successful in doing just that. Only through demoralizing the Dongs, only by making them feel ashamed of what they were, did we succeed in preparing them psychologically for the Great Capitulation which led to the Great Succession. Why, in shame, Charles Atlas himself—famous for kicking sand in people's faces at the beach—became Charlotte Atlas and was thenceforth admired for the Grable-like beauty of her legs, or so it is claimed. And now persons like Miz Mandalay, perhaps unwittingly, with the same kind of misguided generosity of spirit that led to the downfall of the Dongs, are doing to us what we did years ago in Pre-Succession days to the Dongs.

"Those who aid subversives, even unwittingly, are themselves subversive, and enemies of the State. If Miz Mandalay were to achieve full control, I have no doubt but that she would turn Atalanta over to the Dongs. Do I detect the odor of the sexual regressive? That's why we must be vigilant, and at the same time take strong action on both fronts—against traitors, and against Dongs." She addressed the Emergency Session of the Univacual Council, with a special word for Miz Mandalay:

"And I suppose you would give in to their demands, Miz Mandalay, and then when the Dongs ask for the right to be delegates you'd give in again—and why not just save us all a great deal of time and turn the hard-won reins of gov-ernnesting over to them right now, I ask you? Why don't we just go back to jock strap rule—back to the rule of— pardon my language—toxic masculine principle, Sandowism—where war is peace? Hey? Answer me that!" She twirled a not completely imaginary mustache and looked contemptuously at Miz Mandalay.

"If Miz Edgahoova were any kind of scholar," Miz Mandalay responded, rising from her seat, her clear, crisp voice ringing with the self-assurance and the apparent lucid-ity of her class (which was top-tone—her mother owned three States), "the Miz would be forced to admit that we have engaged in thirty minor counteractions and two major ones since the Succession. It is to our shame that we have proven to be as violent as were the Dongs when they ran things."

"Bah! Rocket Smoke! More violent!" cried Jaye Edgahoova, removing a spaceshoe and banging her rostrum top. She then grabbed from her satchel a copy of Plutarch's *Lives,* which she had been reading for the purpose of glean-ing advice on warfare, and now she lifted it and brought it down on her rostrum-top with the explosive sound of a cherry bomb. "We got to meet force wid force," she cried, falling back, as she sometimes did, especially when angered, on the rough, Jerseyish language of her youth. Out of common stock, she had fought her way to the top, tooth and nail, both feet forward.

"Dose Dames—" her aide took her by the sleeve and tugged. Her indiscretion noted, Miz Edgahoova renewed her attack with greater caution and better diction: "Those Yellow Mize were sneaking into our territory. If Miz

Mandalay were as much of a Statesmiz as she is a scholar, she would know that our economy depends on the Tesla windmills of those Islands. What were we supposed to do—stand by and let them take them?"

"An extremely Dong-like argument" said Miz Mandalay, totally unaware of the bigotry in her statement.

"Oh no you don't," cried Jaye Edgahoova. "Just because you don't want to dirty your hands with jobs like that, and you let me make all the dirty decisions, don't mean you have a right to identify me with Dong-think. The Yellows was already shipping our oil away when my skyfleets creamed 'em."

"It could have been settled with reason," said Miz Mandalay with an unfortunate tinge of smugness.

"Reason!" Miz Edgahoova was boiling over. "Before we even opened fire the Yellows had shot down six ten-billion dollar Crawford Spikeheel rocketeers! Reason, she says!" Miz Edgahoova's aide tugged at her sleeve again. Miz Edgahoova pulled her arm free.

"I don't care," she shouted, pounding the rostrum top with her spaceshoe for emphasis, "I've said it before, and I'll say it right now, before this august body, those Yellows are tough titties. They'd have creamed us if I hadn't acted in time—or if you'd had your way."

At which several Yellow Mize scrambled to their feet and exited in a flurry, causing a general stir.

"Now you see what you've done!" cried Miz Mandalay. "You've offended the visiting representatives from the Mainland of Mizmou!"

"Bitches!" muttered Miz Edgahoova. "Them Yellow bitches!"

"Mize! Mize! Please! Order!" called Miz Mandalay. "Now then, it's time to hear the reports."

132

Miz Edgahoova, who had slumped back into her contour double-cheek cup, now jumped back to her feet. "I called for this emergency session," she cried, "and I'll call for the reports."

"Then please do," said Miz Mandalay. "Do let's get down to business and then some facts."

"If it's facts that this assembly wants, I've got 'em," claimed Miz Edgahoova. "As I was saying, them demonstrations must be stopped—"

"Facts, Miz Edgahoova," said Miz Mandalay coolly, "I called for facts."

"It's a fact that these demonstrations have been undermining the morale of the ruling Mize—that's a fact!"

"Speak for yourself; I was never more confident. These are great times to live in. Truly turbulent!"

Miz Edgahoova's rejoinder of "Balls," the filthiest of all words was spoken in such a low tone that none of the delegate Mize were sure they'd heard it. Still, it sent an electric thrill through the assembly. Miz Mandalay, fearing to reprimand Miz Edgahoova's language, also not certain of it, blushed to her tiny toes, but remained tight-lipped.

"The truth is," said Miz Edgahoova, "these are dangerous times. I repeat, the other day I told my class at the Female Bureau of Investigation that revolution begins in peaceful protest. As soon as the Dongs see that we are not willing to relinquish our power to them, they'll take active steps to steal it from us, just as the revolutionary libbies of the Succession did to them. That's politics! That's life! That's facts!"

"No speeches, please," interrupted Miz Mandalay. "No political theories—just facts."

"O.K., then I call as my first witness Miz Rabble-Mead, who has been working closely with me on this issue. As you all know, Miz Rabble-Mead is Ministmiz of

Depopulation—also well known for her work in anthropological sperm confusion—"

Miz Edgahoova nodded, smiled graciously, and extended a hand for Miz Rabble-Mead. "Miz Rabble-Mead," she announced.

A pleasant-looking, rather tubby little Miz who had produced several Say-screen docus on the mating habits of the ancient Rednecks, tumbled to her feet, saying:

"Mind you, Gentlemize, I am a scientist, and therefore it behooves me to be Harvardly objective. I stand with the truth. Hem, hem! Now then. There is no doubt but that there is great unrest among the Dongs. I have here a list of complaints that has come into my commission's possession from the four corners of the Universe—which we are currently repairing—hem, hem! I have been asked by the Left Honorable Miz Edgahoova to read these complaints before this Assembly. I shall do so. But I wish it to be understood that I draw no conclusions.

"Number one . . . Three days ago, in the state of Femina, a large group of radical left-wing piece-marching Dongs paraded before the Mansion of Dr. Brothers-Marx—known to the Universe as Groucha of Femina, who owns said state—marched, I say, in full erection, and with marigolds jutting from the mouths of their erected members, carrying banners and placards bearing such legends as WE WANT A PIECE! and USE US, DON'T ABUSE US! This march was broken up by the Honorable Miz Edgahoova's Tactical Shrike Squads. Unfortunately, these wonderfully combative units were later accused by members of the radical media of having used more force than was necessary—of roughly pulling marigolds out and deliberately breaking off some frozen members . . ."

"Get on to the next report," cried Jaye Edgahoova.

"Please go on," said Miz Mandalay.

"Well," went on the scientific Miz Rabble-Mead blithely, "Tactical Shrikes were accused of clubbing the erected members of the protesting Dongs; even of knocking the flowers from the muzzles of some of their members and trampling them—the flowers—underfoot with obvious glee—"

"Perhaps," said Miz Edgahoova, "they were a *little* too zealous. But they have a hard job. It's not easy to keep the Dongs down."

"This was just one incident reported in the past few days," Miz Rabble-Mead went on. "In Marthatown it was reported that small bands of Dongs gathered near the rotunda before a bronze statue of Edna St. Vincent Millay, whom the protesters felt had treated Dongs as mere sexual objects. They made reference to her sonnet, beginning: 'What lips my lips have kissed, and where and why;' which goes on to say that she had forgotten.

"The Dongs began by discarding their traditional dogsuit uniforms and shaving off their pubic hair. They then piled the pubic hair into a great heap at the foot of the statue of Miz Millay and set it afire while chanting—

> We've minds to use and more
> We've been sexual objects too long
> Our minds as well as our backs are strong
> We're not ashamed, we're not ashamed,
> We're not ashamed anymore
> The Dong, the Dong, the *Dong!*
> The Dong with the luminous nose!

Unfortunately, the Tactical Shrike Squad arrived on the scene too late to prevent any of this—"

"I tell you," cried Jaye Edgahoova, "we're flooded with requests—"

"Here's another," Miz Rabble-Mead went on, "from, of all places, Papal-Land. Perhaps this is the most significant of all. This report, though I hasten to add, *unconfirmed,* has it that in Papal-Land—certainly the *last* place . . . that the Dongs have been burning their jockstraps!"

"I think they look kinda cute that way," whispered a back-bench Ultra-blue to her colleague. "I like the way they bounce when they walk."

"Shhh!" shushed her associate, suppressing a giggle.

"—And using such cries," Miz Rabble-Mead hastened on, "as 'Dong Power,' 'Empower the Tower,' and 'A Piece of the Action'!"

"We've all grown quite used to such vulgarities," put in Miz Mandalay, trying to subdue the assemblage, which had grown loud and lusty. "Please go on."

"Well, here's another. Only yesterday, only a few blocks from this building, three young Dongs quietly infil-trated Mary Sorley's Old Tea House, and managed to get served."

An offended roar came from the Anglo-Irish, Molly Maguires, the Lassies of Ire, contingent.

"I saw a piece," said an Ultra-blue Representative, "the other night on the Joanie Carson's Nightie Show, where they had Huley Heftem of the Playmiz Clubs—and they asked her what she thought of Dong-lib, and you know what she said?"

"What?"

"She said: 'We've got nothing against Dongs—as long as they don't take off their Donkey tails and sit down with the customers. She had brought a Donkey Dong with her who just sat there with a stupid smile on his face, and Hefty ogled him and said, 'A Dong's place is in a heart-shaped bed.' It was so funny."

"Shhh!"

136

Miz Rabble-Mead went on: "—and these are only a minute number of serious offences. But, mind, I am trying to be subjective."

"Well, if Miz Rabble-Mead, as a scientist, finds that it's impossible to draw a conclusion, I, as a Statesmiz have an opposite duty," said Jaye Edgahoova. "The situation is dangerous to the tranquility of the State. I propose immediate forceful suppression of the Dongs. Come on, let's put 'em in their place!"

"Violence solves nothing," said Miz Mandalay. "Are you drunk?"

"Balls!"

"Miz Edgahoova!"

"*Balls*, I said—and balls I meant. Let my Tactical Shrike Squads loose on 'em. They'll scatter like sperm."

A little later, Miz Mandalay left the council, her faction sadly defeated. Miz Edgahoova had proved once again what she had always known to be true: Reason has no chance in a competition with Energy. Jaye Edgahoova had won.

"Now," she said wrathfully, after the council room had nearly cleared, "when I get my mitts on the ringleader of those Dongs, that big dick Resurgius, I'll nail his balls to the wall. I'll teach him he can't steal my sexmiz."

Some few ears were cupped, but the brains attached remained mystified.

3

THE KIDNAPPING OF MIZ MANDALAY

Revolution is the affair of logical lunatics.
—Wallace Stevens

"Miz Mandalay looks angry," said one of the Butcher-birds, the elite, degenderit Secret Service Shrikes whose duty it was to guard the Statesmize, as Miz Mandalay rocketed from the Assembly Room.

"We'd better be on our little toesies. When she's in a conniption tizzy she's hard to keep up with." Her two companions nodded knowingly.

"She's got her five-inch spikes on," said one of them, "they'll slow her down."

"I hope she doesn't go kissing through the crowd, spreading joy," said the other.

"No chance," said the one in charge, "she's pissed."

"Cripes, what an ass she's got!" said the second. "They rub against each other and keep coming up like an upside-down heart, if you look at it the right way."

"And look at them anti-sex objects bounce," said the third, as Miz Mandalay flew by.

"Come on," said the one in charge, "we gotta keep up with her."

Miz Mandalay was already out the door.

When the Secret Service Shrikes hit the street, Miz Mandalay was wriggling into the back seat of her auto-chauffeured limousine, a pale pink Camille 3000.

Suddenly all bordello broke loose.

Three wobbly, crazy-looking superdupermodelmize, their makeup smeared, made a lunging hobble for the car.

"Hey, you!" cried the Secret Service Shrike in charge. "What do you think you're doing?"

"Them are Dongs!" cried the second.

"Sure, look at those scrawny legs!" cried the third.

"No worse than yours!" cried another. "But modelmize don't have cods."

But before the Secret Service Shrikes could think what action to take, the three Dongs, who were dressed like high-fashion superdupermodelmize, had pulled Miz Mandalay from the love seat of her Camille 3000, and were now hustling the struggling Statesmiz into the wicker basket of a gigantic balloon, that looked for all the Universe like a golden condom.

"What's that on the top of the balloon?" asked the stunned second Secret Service Shrike.

"Tassels?" suggested the third, doubtfully.

"Feathers," said the Shrike in charge. "It's a French tickler."

"Cripes!" cried the second.

"Wow!" cried the third. "It looks like one of them ancient Quaint Wieners. I saw one in the museum of natural history."

"But it's golden," cried another. "Must be mustard all over it."

"Where are you taking me?" Miz Mandalay cried from the basket.

"To Resurgius," said the one with the bad hairy legs, the ugliest of the imitation superdupermodelmize. His green lipstick was smeared and he had at least ten o'clock shadow.

And up, up, and away, went the beautiful balloon. But at first the ride wasn't a smooth one. The glass canyons of the great state of Atalanta are deep and dark, and there is a long way to go before you get to the seductive sulphur of the sky.

Once the balloon caught in the towering marquee of the Porno Palace, and Miz Mandalay noted that "Little Men" was on the bill. She didn't have time to see what the second feature was, for the ugly Dong wearing the green lipstick had pushed them free. Up, up they soared, the sky above, the crowd below.

"Why don't they do something?" cried Miz Mandalay. By "they" she meant the three, now tiny, Secret Service Shrikes, who looked almost as if they were waving her good-bye.

Finally the great golden balloon cleared the tops of the skyscrapers and sailed out over the River Slime, buffeted occasionally by a sky full of commercial drones. Miz Mandalay could see the great LaMer Turnpike off in the distance, and behind her even the brightest lights of the city were fading, and for all Miz Mandalay knew she would never see them again. One crystal tear formed in each beautiful violet eye.

"What do you mean to do to me?" she asked the one in green lipstick.

"That's up to Resurgius."

"What's he like?"

"He's the greatest Dong in the Universe."

"How does he command such worship from his followers?" Miz Mandalay asked, trying to learn something of the Dong whose prisoner she had become.

"Why he gave us back our pride," said the Dong. "He showed us that Dong was beautiful." At which the other two Dongs in the basket burst enthusiastically into the chant—

We've minds to use and more—

But green lipstick quickly ordered them to shut up. "We'll have no more say until we arrive at our destination."

And so the roar of the passing drones was the only sound Miz Mandalay heard until the balloon began to descend far out over the LaMer Turnpike.

"Why that's the old Maidenform factory down there," cried Miz Mandalay. It still gave her a slight sensation of pride to see the remains of a Dong-supported industry in deflation.

The balloon settled, with a few bounces, to the roof.

"All out," ordered green lipstick, and Miz Mandalay climbed out of the basket.

"Where to?" she asked, rather anticipating her meeting with the great Dong leader, Resurgius.

"This way," she was told, and followed.

Green lipstick led her down a stairwell and into a huge, long loft-room at the far end of which sat a Dong, whom she assumed to be the mighty Resurgius, and none other than Miz Bet, whose month-ago disappearance had been the trigger of Jaye Edgahoova's wrath.

Resurgius and Miz Bet sat like two monarchs of old, side by side, each in a padded inverted cup of the ten-foot wide white plastic Maidenform bra that had once been a sign on the roof of the building. Around and before them, but with all eyes turned on Miz Mandalay, were at least twenty couples, Dongs and Cunnies, gathered like a court, whom Miz Mandalay rightly took to be Resurgius' top aides. It was humiliating for her to have to walk the long red carpet toward that perverted group of naturals. "He's trying to psyche me," she thought to herself, and walked handsomely forward. When she got close enough the court opened a path for her and she was brought directly before Resurgius and Miz Bet. To the latter, Miz Mandalay said:

"So, it's true then. You have gone over. You have become a Cunnie. How disgraceful. A Miz of your rank!"

"Don't *Miz* me," said Miz Bet. "My name is Beth. You will use that name when addressing me, and when appropriate."

"Beth! What a name! It sounds positively Elizabethan," said Miz Mandalay, in a show of bravado. But she *was* a bit awed. "And I suppose this is the great Dong himself."

"This is Resurgius," said Beth. The Dong, a huge, bronzed, gold-and-flame-headed fellow remained silent, and this had the effect of making Miz Mandalay even more nervous and uncertain than before.

"Can't he talk?" she said. "After all, I am a Univacual leader, and have the right to expect respectful treatment."

But the flame-haired Dong's green eyes only glittered mischievously, if through his hornrims, darkly. Miz Mandalay turned her own eyes to Beth.

"Is this the kind of life you want?"

Beth was a busty, satin-skinned brunette with wonderful calves and long green eyes which Miz Mandalay guessed were only plastics, and which she now slid across her face to aim at what she saw as Resurgius' classic profile. Hypnotized by love, what she saw was an "R" chested super suit, made of red, white and blue plastic, red caped, and from which at the collar emerged Resurgius' stalk of a neck, and a head actually resembling Woody Allen's—an ancient movie star—wearing a pair of hornrimmed glasses.

"What do *you* think, baby?" Miz Bet said with a sexy smirk.

"How long have you been involved in this sort of thing?" said Miz Mandalay, ignoring Miz Bet's facial implications.

"Since the beginning," said Beth proudly. "Why do you think I ever had anything to do with that sow, Edgahoova? It was only in order to get my position in Dong Pop. I knew that from there I would be able to work under cover to stir the limp, demoralized Dongs to revolutionary erection. I first got the idea a few years ago. It occurred to me that if someone could induce a hardon in the Dongs, that would last for at least four hours, they could be a tremendous source of power. Then, a little later, one day at the office, I got the craves and sent out for a Dong. They sent Resurgius up to me and I liked his style, as who wouldn't! and so the next time I got the craves I asked that they send me the same Dong. Pretty soon, in the after-say and shared electronic vape, I came to see that he was the Dong that I was looking for to lead the coup. Brawn and brains! He and I together have planned everything—all those protests that had old Edgahoova in such a fit. She'd tell me everything, so I always knew how to counteract whatever action she might take. I used to laugh behind the old bag's back. But I *have* had my problems."

"Yes," said Resurgius, his voice like low drums, his speech like a tympanic tongue, "Beth means that she had had some difficulty convincing me of the wisdom of using actual force. Fundamentally, you see, I'm a pacifist, a lover—especially with my plastic Resurgius suit on—which has many push-button valves."

"Yes," said Beth, "he had been rather overshamed at Shame-school, unfortunately, and I had a hard time of it convincing him that force must be met with force, as Jaye Edgahoova so well taught me. Look at those muscles!"

143

"Yes," said Resurgius, a little sadly, "the white feather in me has had to admit that force must be employed if we are to win our goal."

"Which is?" asked Miz Mandalay, sharp, little ears aperk.

"Well," said Resurgius, "my original goal was equality, but—"

"But," said Beth, "I have showed him that it is a political fact of life among us simple simians, that there are oppressors and oppressed—"

"And if you don't want to be oppressed—" broke in Resurgius—

"—then you must oppress," Beth finished.

"And so, reluctantly, we have taken to the use of force," said Resurgius.

"This is very depressing," said Miz Mandalay, "and I'm your first victim."

"You are our first victim," said Resurgius, "but you needn't remain one. You might consider joining us."

"Never!"

"Very well, but the invitation will remain open."

"And in the meantime," said Beth, "we should be able to get some great concessions from the Univacual Council for the promise of your return."

"Of course, you will never return me to them . . . ."

"Of course not."

"But if you were to join us," said Resurgius, "we naturally would still be able to get what we want. They need never know that you aren't being held forcibly."

"She doesn't *want* to join us, Resurgius, didn't you hear her?" There were sparks at Beth's temples, and her eyes blazed emerald.

"I just thought—"

144

"I'm beginning to see what you're thinking," snapped Beth.

"She's right," said Miz Mandalay staunchly, "I'll never join. You are all enemies of Atalanta Mizstate, and you'll come to a bloody end when Miz Edgahoova's Tactical Police Shrikes catch up with you." At which threat, Beth only sniffed as if smelling something unpleasant.

"You'll see," Miz Mandalay added weakly.

"She has spunk," said a Dong member of the Court, off to the left of Miz Mandalay.

"That's what gives her her leadership qualities," said his Cunnie. "But if she only knew what she was missing," she added coyly, looking up into her Dong's eyes, which were awkwardly crossed, looking down, back.

"What I'd like to know is," said Miz Mandalay, "why are you telling me all this? And also, I'd like to know what's in it for you, Miz Bet? You're from a good background and you had a top post. Are you, perish the thought, *in love* with this—this *Dong*? You can have all you want of him or a hundred like him, you know. Why on earth do you want to make yourself his slave?"

"She is *not* my slave," said Resurgius. "If anything, I am her slave. But there'll be no talk of slavery. Beth is my wife."

"Wife!" cried Miz Mandalay. "Have you no respect, to use such a filthy pre-Succession word? There is no such thing as a—what you said, don't you know that? It's against the law."

"Resurgius is the law here," said Beth, "and I am indeed his wife—wife, wife, wife!— and to me it is the most wonderful word in the world.

"As to your questions—we are telling you about ourselves because Resurgius, who is the kindest Dong in the Universe," with which she gave him a wifely side-wise smile, "hoped that you would see the light, and join us. I had no doubt that you would not. You are all reactionaries, even you, who claim to be such a liberal, when there's any question of losing power. For me, I had a father, a real one, not something from the sperm bank or the vulcanization chamber, and though I never knew him, I have had my dreams of what he was like. I picture him—"

"Never mind that," said Miz Mandalay. "Everybody at the top knows about your mother's indiscretion."

"I picture him," Beth went on, "with white hair, standing in the kitchen before an old-fashioned raystove, baking me an apple pie."

"Beth," Resurgius nudged her.

"Hem!" she cleared her voice. "Anyway, my sympathies have always been with the Dongs. There's an old song that my great-grandmother used to sing—"*I enjoy being a girl.*"

"Rotten old pre-Succession time," said Miz Mandalay.

"I know, but I love it," said Beth dreamily. "I'm an old-fashioned girl at heart, and they've pumped me so full of estrogen that I sag." She looked at Resurgius. "I swing and sway."

"And ambition," said Miz Mandalay, "the desire for ultimate power, couldn't have anything to do with it, I suppose."

"Naturally, I'd like to rule the Universe, be the Queen of all I survey. Wouldn't anybody? First level psychology explains that, how deep inside of us the only way we can feel truly safe is to be in control. You're just the same."

"Pooh!"

"Oh yes, it's true. You've got it in you, too."

"I suppose it's a throwback to your early disgrace. Very unfortunate. But do you suppose that this Dong is going to let *you* run things. He'll have all the power, *if* you succeed."

"And I'll have him, which is the same thing as having the power. I can withhold sex and make him do my bidding. He is a Dong, after all. You love me, don't you, my dear Dong?"

"Deedy, I do, but much of what you two are saying is over my head. I'm just a simple guy."

"Sorry, darling. Now what do you propose we do with our guest?"

"Take her to the padding room and feed her. She's a bit too lean for my taste."

"Take her away," cried Beth, and then added, "and for Cripe's sake, get her a bra—the Howard Hughes Double Derrick."

4

MOONLIGHT SONATA

The Howard Hughes Double Derrick was a torture device designed by the pre-Succession Dong for the ancient movie star Jane Russell, whom the famous Dong engineer had apparently hated. It caused the anti-sex objects to be pressed upward toward the chin in an extremely uncomfortable fashion. Beth's insistence that Miz Mandalay wear that horrid instrument of torture, which had been found, moth-eaten and faded, but with wiring and padding intact, in a bin of specialty brassieres, was indicative of her distaste for their kidnap victim.

Try as he might, enemy that she was, Resurgius could not feel the same rancor toward Miz Mandalay that Miz Bet apparently felt.

Perhaps it was her beauty. Miz Mandalay resembled a relentlessly blossoming female figure from a Frank Frazetta painting that he had seen in a secret collection of banished art. Much as he tried to contain himself, she steamed his hornrims and made him drool like a baby. After watching a few days of her suffering in the padding room, he relented in Beth's name and told Miz Mandalay that she might remove the Howard Hughes Double Derrick. To be sure that his orders were carried out, he stood and watched as she did so. The removal of the torture device prompted in him an even greater generosity of spirit, and he went on to tell Miz Mandalay that she might have the freedom of the top two floors of the five-storey factory, and also of the roof, but she was warned that escape was impossible.

The roof had an eight-foot-high chain-link fence around it, for in the pre-Succession days the factory workers had used it for games and exercise, and all the windows down below were heavily gated. The lower floors made dormitories for a crack battalion of Resurgius' troops and their warrior Cunnies, who marched with old-fashioned electric harpoons. The basement had been converted into a combined garage—one basement door ran out onto the slope of a hill—arsenal, and storage room for supplies.

Miz Mandalay decided to partake of the night air, and climbed to the roof. All the beautiful, dull bronze stars were out, for the month was Mae. Many lovely shades of smoke filled the air with the bracing scent of sulphur, and one could see the parti-colored signal lights on the half-moon's dark portion. It reminded her of the article she'd recently read in "Kosmo." *At the Meat Market in the Mall on the Moon, there are no cuts of dead animals, only meat, muscles and organs, developed from cells in a dish. Rumps, shanks, and livers that have never had a body. Vegetarians are in a state of consternation. Should such meat be condemned? But no animal died in its production. The meat is developed without nervous connection, so there has never been pain. There has never been life, in a sense, for none of this meat has had a head (sorry, brains are not manufactured). Should something be done? It is alive, in a sense, but its life must be a profound dimness, an almost nothingness. The Modern Meat Packers Association insists, on a Sartre-like nothingness. Skin, and fur, of course, are developed (grown) in the same manner. There are no animals, merely*

149

yards of skin and fur, fur of all kinds: mink, ermine, seal, sable. But you do not buy them at the Meat Market in the Mall on the Moon, you buy them at the Fur Coat Fair in the Mall on the Moon, where you can also purchase birdless feathers, and alligator shoes from alligator skin grown without legs or heads on huge trays in factories in Orlando and Boca Raton. Horns and tusks of all kinds can be bought, whole or powdered, at the Horn and Tusk Shop in the Mall on the Moon, and not one horn or tusk, whole or powdered, has had a concomitant animal: no elephant has been poached, no deer has been slaughtered for its antlers, no moose has been shot, no wild boar has been knifed, arrowed, or clubbed. But they are all represented at the Horn and Tusk Shop in the Mall on the Moon.

Miz Mandalay hopelessly wished that she were at some resort on the Sea of Tranquility tonight, instead of being held a prisoner in an old, defunct brassiere factory. She wished she were eating an ancient Quaint Weiner, made of disgusting bad cholesterol, dripping fat, smeared with mustard and covered with sauerkraut, as people did happily once upon a time, at Coney Island, as she had seen pictures of in the ancient history books reproduced from the 2075 Giant Kloud, the Giant Kloud which was now so ancient and so full that nobody understood the early stuff that was in it; also a real Chesterfield cigarette and not a stupid humped Camel Vape. She was certain that nothing that came from the Meat Market at the Mall on the Moon could taste as good as a Quaint Weiner or a real smoke. Somewhere deep inside she was just an old-fashioned girl.

She wished now that at the last Economic Studies Conference she had voted for more funds for Poverty, so that this building and many others like it, that stood like ghosts of a bygone era about the fringes of Atalanta, might have been razed or perhaps converted for low income animal life or vegetable pod factories.

She couldn't help wondering why, for all their work, they had still been unable to get rid of poverty. Certainly her own mother had done her best to do just that in the State that she owned—Hollystate, which, unfortunately, was in danger of sinking in the sea, thus putting a final end to the film industry and its three remaining stars, who wouldn't leave—the State that would someday be her own. Her mother, Miz Nansome, took as much money as she could from the middle-class Mize of her state and gave it to the starving tent people—O the grapes of wrath—and the Central State pursued the same policy under Governor Noisome. Somehow, it seemed that poverty just went hand in hand with progress. Well, that wasn't really her field of expertise, and she had no right to think of it. She cleared her head.

"Ah parti-colored moon in the lovely, sulphurous heavens, you above all know that there is a tide in the affairs of Dongs, which, taken at the full, leads on to fortune. I have studied and prepared, and my time has come . . . ."

It was Resurgius! He stood alone, not twenty feet ahead, looking for all the Universe like an ancient statue of Eugen Sandow, pale, except for his glinting hornrims, against the night.

"Oh, shine on, shine on harvest moon up in the sky. I ain't had no lovin' since January, February, June or July—" He was singing.

"Ahem!" went Miz Mandalay, her natural good manners requiring that she make her presence known.

"Oh," said Resurgius, startled. "I—"

"You were talking to yourself, or singing, maybe." She walked up to him, thinking, "what a curious creature! I should like to know more about him! What shoulders! And

151

what a small neck and what a big head. And what big glasses, and why the cape?"

"What are you then," asked Miz Mandalay, "a Say-screen that talks even if no one is present?"

"Yes," said Resurgius, turning to meet her, "it's a curious habit acquired early, when I had only myself for a friend."

"Then you had a Dong for a friend," said Miz Mandalay, wittily. "That's even more curious, don't you think?"

"You think so little of us, then?"

"Not so little, perhaps. But when I think of Dongs, I think of pre-Succession days. I think of the plight of Mize like my grandmother, and her mother, who led such lives of terrible hardship and virtual enslavement under the iron thumb of the Dongs."

"Your grandmother's husband, you mean, and her mother's husband. They, too, led hard lives, and solved their problems as they could. After your grandmother washed the stinky clothes in a washing machine, your grandfather took the laundry in a basket and hung it on a line with clothes-pins. They suffered too. Their thumbs were raw."

Miz Mandalay looked at the giant's poor little hands. "But see how things have changed since the Succession—"

"Yes, now Dongs are virtual slaves; I see that nothing has changed but the generations. Today there are masters and slaves just as always, and women are the masters."

"Well, I myself have fought in council to raise the position of the Dongs."

"Yes, you are a liberal, like my grandfather, Dr. Spank—"

"*He* was your fore-Dong?"

"Indeed he was. It was he, as you seem to be aware, who was the great Dong champion of Mize rights. I remember often how he would call himself a pig. If you will recall your history, you'll remember that it was he who was the pioneer of the Shame-schools."

"I do remember something about him in that line, but the main credit for the Shame-school principle is usually conceded to be that of Carrie Nation."

"I assure you that it was my mother's father's concept. He wanted the Universe to be a good place for his daughter to grow up in. He never disciplined her, and unfortunately she rebelled against his shapelessness and became a gartered Cunnie. She was one of the first after the Succession. She was rather wild, obviously. A great fan of that ancient actor, John Wayne. In those days, if you'll remember, the Cunnies were known as Trampers. She was one of the first Trampers, wore skirts and everything. Of course, if it hadn't been for her slap-happy madness, I shouldn't be here today, and perhaps the Universe would not be on the brink of revolution."

"You really mean to pursue this revolt of the Dongs, then. . ."

"I have decided to do so."

"You'll never succeed, you know. You might have been able to deal with me, but you've made the wrong move by this kidnapping. Jaye Edgahoova will attack, tooth and nail, both feet forward."

"How can she attack when we have you for a hostage?"

"Bah! She'll let you kill me if you wish, then she'll have supreme power. Do you think my death would bother her in the least? It is only I that stand between her and total control. All you have done by kidnapping me is to give her the excuse she needed to annihilate you."

"Will she be so ruthless?"

"Absolutely."

153

"But why then did Beth, who knows Edgahoova so well, advise me to take this step?"

"I have been thinking about that myself, and I think I have the answer."

"Say, please."

"I doubt that you will believe me. . . ."

"I repeat; say, please."

"You said that you at first believed in principles of pacifism."

"I did, until I saw that they were futile."

"Think, then, Resurgius, you are involved with a Miz possessed of a demon."

"She's not like that."

"Isn't she? I offer this possibility, dear Dong, for your consideration: Miz Bet—"

"Beth."

"All right, then, Beth is fully aware that this action which she has advised you to take will bring an attack by Jaye Edgahoova in its wake. She is staking everything on it. She is afraid that you'll fall back into pacifism if you have time to think of what bloodshed might be ahead. She is gambling that you will be forced into open war, that you'll be able to repulse Edgahoova's first onslaught—she probably still has spies in Edgahoova's employ who will tip her as to what that Miz will do, so that you will be prepared—and then, that you will reign supreme in the counterattack."

"If what you say is true, my Beth is treacherous."

"I doubt that her treachery will stop there, Resurgius."

"What do you mean?"

"I mean that, if you are successful—but you won't be—as soon as you assume control, you will find yourself chewing poisoned gum."

Resurgius stood, his large bronzed forehead furrowed in thought, lifting his hornrims from his eagle beak; then his forehead smoothed and his eyes sparkled with eked intelligence behind his hornrims.

"And earlier you warned her of me," he said. "It couldn't be that you are trying to divide and conquer, could it?"

"But of course I am," said Miz Mandalay, lightly. "Still, what I say is true. Eventually, one of you will turn against the other."

"I can see that you don't know what love is," said Resurgius.

"Love—between a Dong and a Miz—it's ludicrous."

"Love is never ludicrous."

"Not between equal Mize, but—"

"Ah, the liberal speaketh—

"I only meant—"

"Listen," said Resurgius, "let me tell you of my love. As a boy, like all boys, I was taught shame. I had to sit for three hours a day before the Say-screen while a Miz told me the errors of my toxic masculine nature. I was taught, just as my grandfather had conceived that the method should be, that I was swinish, brutish, insensitive, cruel, stupid, gross, with no capacity for fineness of sentiment or depth of emotion. I was told that even my organs felt as nothing compared with a woman's G-spot. In short, I was taught to hang my head and walk ashamed. I grew up during the period of severest suppression, right after the Great Succession. But one thing kept my spirit alive—a few lines of a poem that I remembered my mother reciting to me. They're by an early American poet named Robert Frost, and they certainly pertained to my grandfather, and therefore were a symbol to me. I don't remember exactly, but they went something like this:

I'm a liberal, you know what that is—
Liberals are people who never take their
Own side in a quarrel."
"Nonsense!"
"Perhaps, but that sustained me, kept the spark of faith in myself alive. It taught me to take my own side against that Say-screen at Shame-school. They saved me from my pacifist tendencies when I was taken to be a gladiator. I kept thinking of my opponent, but what good will it do to let him kill me? I have as much right to live as he. Or why do I not? And I could think of no reason. After all, it was *I* inside of me, someone with as much of a claim on life as he."
"That's the root of war."
"Yes, it is: circumstance and survival."
"Ugly."
"No, beautiful. Tragic but beautiful. Then I was taken from gladiatorial service, after sustaining a serious wound, and placed out to stud. As Beth told you, it was on a crave call that I met her. Which brings us back to love, for it was she who taught me the meaning of the word."
"Gratitude, not love, is the word for it."
"Well then, perhaps—have it as you will. But try to think what it meant to me when, instead of the usual treatment, she treated me like a person with a soul. Once, during the after-say, she read to me from a very ancient book called *Plutarch's Lives*, how a slave named Spartacus lead a revolt against his masters. She read how a snake coiled itself on his face as he lay asleep, and his wife, who was with him, and was a kind of prophetess, declared that it was a sign portending great and formidable power to him. I remember how the story stirred something in me, and excited me, and I fell asleep dreaming of it, and how suddenly the dream became so real that I could feel that snake upon my own face,

and I jumped up to find that Beth had truly placed a small asp across my face that fell into my lap when I sat up, and, though I had been terrified, still I knew then that I had a destiny—for I had not been bitten—and that it was Beth who would help me to fulfill it. So you see, I knew that I loved her, and she me."

"You were grateful, Resurgius," said Miz Mandalay, genuinely touched by the story. "Perhaps we have been too hard on the Dongs," she added after a reflective moment. "But, you see, we have feared just such an enterprise as you now propose to undertake. It has always been my feeling that we should have given the Dongs the vote. It would have been a healthy channel wherein to release their frustrations and would have meant nothing, anyway."

"No," said Resurgius, "from your view, I believe that it was better that you didn't. A little freedom will always lead to the demand for more. My grandfather, Doctor Spank, made that mistake—giving the Mize that freedom—and I have paid for it with a life of slavery."

"Now you sound like Jaye Edgahoova—like a Conservative."

"A Conservative keeps what she's got for as long as she can, which certainly seems more like a natural impulse."

"You poor Dong, your mind, your soul, have been corrupted—"

"By society."

"By Beth."

"I've told you that I love her."

"Yes, you have, you poor Dong."

"But wait! As I looked at you in this beautiful sulphurous light, as I've listened to your commanding alto voice, something has come over me, possessed me. I want to sing:

157

Oh sweet and lovely
Lady be good,
Oh lady be good to me—"

"So," said Beth, stepping suddenly from the shadows behind them, "I had the craves and went looking for you, and couldn't find you anywhere. And here I find you on the roof conspiring, as it appears, with the enemy, and romancing her!"

"Oh, Beth my love, Miz Mandalay and I were just—"

"There are no Mize here," Beth interrupted vehemently, "she's just plain Mandy now."

"Mandy!" cried Miz Mandalay indignantly. "How dare you! You were nothing but a third rank official until that fool Edgahoova got a crush you. I have hundreds like you under me."

"Yes," said Beth, "but you're dancing to my music now, my fair Miz. And Mandy you'll be from this day forth. I've a mind to have you locked in the corset room and fed nothing but sliced plastic and radioactive milk. What have you been doing, filling this poor Dong's head with a lot of lies? What's she been saying, Resurgius?"

"Love . . . love . . ."

"Answer me, you big fool!"

"We have been talking about the lights on the moon—see how prettily they spell out the names of products. Look, look now; what does it say? One Calorie, is it?"

In spite of herself, Miz Mandalay wished she could cover a bit for Resurgius, protect him.

"What are you trying to do to my Dong? Turn his head?"

"You've done a pretty fair job of that yourself," Miz Mandalay rejoined. "You've got the poor creature thinking that he can become the super Dong of the universe. Don't you know you're riding him for a terrible fall? He's going to be deeply hurt when he sees that he's incompetent."

"Why, don't tell me you believe your own propaganda. He's got twice your mental capacity."

"Then it's you who should be careful."

"She has nothing to fear from me," said Resurgius.

"She's trying to turn us against each other," said Beth.

"How could I do that?" rejoined Miz Mandalay. "A Dong and an Accidental should make a perfect pair."

"So, you'd throw that up at me, would you?"

Suddenly—perhaps it was Resurgius' hurt, green eyes—they looked green in this sulphurous air and behind the dancing light of his hornrims—that touched her, but Miz Mandalay felt ashamed.

"I'm sorry," she said, looking at Resurgius, whose eyes had teared-up. "Perhaps I shouldn't have said that."

"You certainly shouldn't have," said Beth. "Now you're going to spend the rest of your little visit in the corset room, and don't say I didn't warn you."

"Oh, Beth," said Resurgius, "I don't think we need—"

"Are you going to overrule me—in front of her?"

"No," said Resurgius, shrugging his massive bronze shoulders, and skulking off to a far corner of the roof. He detested scenes.

And so it came to pass that Miz Mandalay was thrown into the corset room, and was left to sleep on a stack of those revolting objects.

5

HER GOVERNMENT IN ACTION

When word was brought back in to the Emergency Session of the Univacual Council, that Miz Mandalay had been kidnapped by three Dongs disguised as superduper-modelmize, and that she had been taken away in a golden condom-like balloon, the members of the Council as a body fairly screeched for reprisals. This was very much to Jaye Edgahoova's taste, and she made good use of all this feline fury.

"Hear me, Mize," she oraged, pebble-mouthed, "the Dongs have stolen from amongst us the flower of our regime, the magnificent Miz Mandalay, whom we all know and love. Who knows but that right now she is being tortured, or even deliberately impregnated"—oohs of hypocritical terror and horror from her auditors—"by the scoundrel Resurgius? First it was our adored Miz Bet. Now it's Miz Mandalay. Who will be next? Me? Thank Sappho for my whiskers. Something must be done!"

Here came great tumult and shouting. There were cries for vengeance. All Dongs, no matter how innocent, should be rounded up and put into detention camps and the Ship of Dongs turned away.

"Great idea!" cried Jaye Edgahoova. "We must learn from history, while not letting it repeat itself. But—I must ask this question—might not such an action bring a reprisal in some form from the Dongs? Dare we to escalate, while they hold Miz Mandalay captive? But then again, dare we not? For what is the life of any one of us as opposed to the life of the Atalanta Mizstate? Sacrifices must be made in times of crisis. I know that if it were I who was being held, I should wish that the vote be for an immediate attack, that I might be made the proud and immortal martyr of freedom— but, do you agree?"

"Yea! Yea! Yea!" came the waves of approval. Vox populi! Vox dei! Long live liberty!

"Then let us withdraw, at this moment of crisis, my citimize, to contemplate the grave implications of our actions, and to make detailed plans of attack."

Volcanic eruptions of applause!

"It has been *your* decision," said Jaye Edgahoova, flushed with success, "I am merely your agent." She slammed her cup on the rostrum and withdrew, leaving the Council hall, and going directly to the Pink House. As she trudged along with her squad of Secret Service Shrikes, she mulled over what she had learned from secret communication with Miz Bet; that Bet had no thought of making any concessions with the Dongs. Edgahoover could trust that dame. As she crossed the lawn, the usual gaggle of reporters from the various news services had spread blankets and were having a tea-party while waiting for a statement from Edgahoova's Press Secretary, Hedy Parsons (also renowned as a pianist and a heavyweight champion weightlifter).

Upon arrival at the Pink House, now a-bustle with activity, she called for her chief of Shrike Police, one Furius, a red-haired ex-barmiz from Hoboken, who was notorious for having bitten off the ears of twenty Dongs. Everyone knew that the story was true, for she kept the ears, in a marinated state, in a gallon pickle jar that stood on her desk in her offices at the Pinafore.

161

"Furius," said Edgahoova, "you are now looking at the absolute Boss of the Universe. The Dongs have played right into my hands. I can wage open war on them and get rid of Miz Mandalay at the same time. I'm thirsty. Get me a Pink Dongly. The kind with the big straws."

"I don't know," said Furius, pouring Edgahoova a drink, "it's too pat."

"What do you mean?" Edgahoova's pointed little red ears twitched.

"Well, why'd da Dongs make such a bad mistake?"

"I say dey was badly advised," said Edgahoova, lapsing into her natural speech.

"Yeah," said Furius, handing her the drink and shoving a skinny office Dong under her legs like a quivering ottoman, "but dat's what I mean. I smell a rat."

"If you mean Bet," said Edgahoova," I don't believe it."

"Yeah, cuz you got a case on her and won't look at da facts when you see 'em."

"You've always been jealous of her."

"O.K., but think about it. Resurgius never did nothin' like this before. This is her work."

"Of course it's her work, you fool. Don't you see that she's set the whole thing up for me. She's on my side."

"Dat's only what you *want* to believe. And if you win, she'll let you believe it. But if you lose, it'll be anudder story."

"She must know that I can't lose. Look at my armies—crawling on their stomachs for me!"

"You see, that's da point! Everybody, including Miz Bet and Resurgius, can look at your armies. But can you look at his? How do *you* know how many Dongs and Cunnies he has under his command? Look how widespread all these incidences have been. And I bet dat's just the tip of the iceboig. They might have spies to tell 'em where and how you'll attack, and they might have a network of millions, scattered through the Universe, to counterattack with. But still, I guess it's possible that they don't know all dongbots are out of commission, even ours, ever since the Univacual Council ruled in ancient times that they'd be immobilized in time of war. You know, Chief, dongbots have always been programmed for pacifism. There's nothing to worry about there."

"True. Course we don't know for sure how much Miz Bet knows or remembers of ancient history."

"She's a scholar, ain't she?"

"Balls! I still say they'd try to strike first."

"Listen, we know from experience dat Resurgius don't work dat way. You know what I tink? I tink Miz Bet wants you to attack, so she can force Resurgius into action."

"Balls!" cried Edgahoova. "I don't believe a word of it."

"You're blinded by love. You've got a superplough on dat witch."

"Shut up and rub my anti-sex objects," said Edgahoova, "I've gotta think."

Seven minutes later, Hedy Parsons called the reporters into the Situation Room for a press conference. Naturally, there was a fine turnout of press Mize—indeed, most of Atalanta's renowned journalists were present, and still brushing tea-cake crumbs from their chins.

There was Sandra Van Orchid, the five-million-bobbit-a-year representative of Public Say-screen and Frieda Unfriendly of Network C.A.T. Nora Postman, the rough-talking, curly-headed femfist, already-famed as a novelist, and now engaged in turning out such timely journalistic spectaculars as the recently best-selling *An Icecube on the*

Sun, was very much present and already sputtering with caustic questions.

From the other side of the political spectrum came the two Wilhelminas; Sneller, of the arch-conservative Univacual Review, and Buckle, host of Public Say-screen's controversial Firing Squad show.

Jacqueline Anders, the Pink House muckraker was in the crowd, Mandalay Restless of the Atalanta *Times*, and Petite Hannabelle, whose firebrand-liberal tabloid column, "Bubbles," had gained her tremendous recent popularity as a somewhat muffled roaring girl.

Oh, yes, they were all there, and they looked tense and exhausted from their long waiting for a scoop. As soon as they were seated, Press Secretary Hedy Parsons made the familiar, solemn statement, "Lady Mize, the Honorable Jaye Edgahoova," and they all got miserably back to their feet, as that formidable Miz strode in and up to the speaker's platform. She was the very picture of energy and decision. Anyone could see that the buck stopped with her (in fact she had several large accounts in Moon banks, and would surely be able to double her assets if the new missile deal went through). Having had little time to make up properly, she was wearing a stern face, with slightly smudged purple lipstick.

"Atalantans," she began immediately, "it is with heavy heart that I come before you this evening to announce a state of crisis in our nation.

"At five o'clock this afternoon, Mae 13, 3000, our Co-Efficient, Most High Miz Mandalay, was, as our best intelligence reports lead us to believe, the victim of a dastardly kidnapping plot, executed with precision and ruthlessness by a group of Dongs disguised as high-fashion superdupermodelmize, to the number of three, whom we believe to be under the leadership of one Resurgius, a

164

former gladiator and call-stud, who has gone underground for the purpose of overthrowing our beloved Motherland.

"Our intelligence services have been working round the clock, for the past few hours, to discover the fate of our beloved leader; but as yet we have received no definite word as to her whereabouts. However, we are expecting word within the hour."

Jaye Edgahoova laid aside the sheet of paper from which she'd been reading, and leveled her little black ingot eyes on the journalists.

"Now there's the end of my prepared statement. I'd like to make a short off-the-cuff comment, however, in addition, before you Mize of the Press begin firing your questions. Off the Cuff—and let me make this perfectly clear— let me add that, though we seek no wider war, we are prepared to use all the vast power at our command to see that Miz Mandalay is returned safely to us and that those double-dealing pinko Dongs—and I hope they are listening—are brought within jabbing distance of the mailed fists of Miz Justice. We will show them no mercy, even if they should return Miz Mandalay unharmed, for they must be taught to ask, not what their country can do for them, but what they can do for their country!

"Now, Mize of the Press, proceed with your most explosive questions, please, and have no fear that I shall shrink from responsible reply. Miz Buckle?"

"I only wished to comment, Miz Edgahoova, that, to employ the oxy-moronic, and not as a mere epigrammatic device, but as an exemplification of my deepest feelings, your manifestation of the timocratical principle of cruel-kindness has caused me to become lachrymose eye for eye, drop for drop, pari-passu, and verbatim ac litteratim, so that you have moved me into a state of expialidocious-supercali-fragilation for the flag."

165

"Well, thanks, Miz Buckle—I guess. How about you, Miz Restless? Got a toughy for me?"

"Well, Miz Edgahoova, you know perfectly well how I've always smugly opposed you—"

"Granted."

"But we can't let Atalanta go down the drain. Not until we've all milked her dry, anyway."

"Granted. I'm glad to see that we agree on something."

"And now I think that during this time of crisis we should all get behind you and support you. I, for one, promise to quit carping until after the crisis."

"Thanks. It took a big Miz to say that."

"I have a question."

"Yes, Norma."

"Well, to quote from that classic work by Ernesta Anyway, *Old Woman on the Ground*, 'Being brave is pressurized grace.'"

"Very true, but what is your question?"

"How'd you like to debate me? Or box?"

"I haven't got time right now, Norma."

"O.K., but have you ever heard of *In Praise of Silly* by Erasamiz?"

"No."

"Well, it's the latest best-seller, and I'm going to debate her, or maybe box her."

"Good, I'll tune in. How about you, Sandy?"

"I think we should get down to cases—the Public wants to know. Does this latest incident tie-up in any way with the disappearance last month of the Chairmiz in charge of Dong Pop, Miz Bet? And if so, how? All of us are familiar with the Pink House scuttlebutt that has it that Miz Bet defected. Would you comment on that?"

166

"Incisive questioning, Sandy. Yes, I'll be glad to comment on that, only to say this, in order to clear that up—so let me make this perfectly clear—Miz Bet—and let me address myself first to her character—is a Miz whose love of country is such that, there can be no doubt, whatsoever, as to the possibility that such an act, insofar as we understand it, but on the other hand, assuming that we have exhausted the possibilities of one, having employed every digit at its command, and on the third hand, all these for the furtherance of truth, as we know it, yet the iniquity of Mize were as easily viewed, in categoric terms, then we should certainly reckon ourselves fortunate, and this State stable. I hope that answers your question, Sandy. I've tried to be specific."

"Thank you."

"Not at all. We certainly desire to have an informed Public, for therein lies the strength of freedom and the free use of strength."

As Miz Edgahoova concluded this observation, she was handed a communiqué by Press Secretary Parsons. She paused to open the paper and read it, then she looked up.

"Gentlemize of the Press, I have just been handed a communiqué of great importance, and I am going to share its contents with you. Contact has been made with representatives of the Dongs, who have asked for certain concessions by our government in return for Miz Mandalay. They make the following demands—which I'll read verbatim.

1. A piece of the action.
2. Suffrage.
3. Right to hold public office.
4. Right to marry.
5. Dismantling of Shame-schools.
6. Impeachment of Jaye Edgahoova.

7. End the war on the dark side of the Moon and bring our girls home.

8. Don't buy any more of those spacejets from your brother-in-law—with our money.

"As you can see, these demands are outrageous and completely unacceptable, and leave us only one course of action. Happily, the Senate and the House of Representatives are on vacation; and, this being clearly a state of emergency, the buck stops with me. Therefore, this day, Mae 13, 3000, a day of infamy, I do declare open and atrocious war upon the Dongs. The little people of this country will fight to the last death-rattle—at home, in their beds, or on the john—and never will your government have owed so much to the acquiescence and stupidity of so many. I thank you."

Furius had a nice double bourbon ready for her leader when the last reporter exited, and Edgahoova entered the little room adjacent the Ovary Office.

"Well," she asked, slamming the door behind her, "how'd it sound, Furius?"

"Chief, that was your finest hour."

"Thanks. How'd you like that part about even if they did return Miz Mandalay unharmed, we'd show them no mercy. That oughta get her throat cut, what?"

"Brilliant, Chief. And the way you fiddled Van Orchid's question about Miz Bet, if she'd brought a tape and played it back slow she couldn't get anything outa that mess."

"Your Chief is on her toes, Furius. Even if you're right about Bet defecting, it helps to keep the ball rolling that they think she was kidnapped too. Then again, if you're wrong about her, no harm's been done."

"Brilliant, Chief. But do you think it was smart to declare war? Wouldn't a surprise attack have been better— a stab in the back?"

"It would have been better if those Dongs thought for a moment that we'd meet their insane demands, but they know perfectly well that the war has started already. They know this is a struggle to the death between me and Resurgius, feet first, tooth and nail. He knows I'm not going to give up everything I've worked for all these years—the suppression of the Dongs, the Great Succession, the fortune I'm making on munitions contracts, all the States I've been able to buy, and don't forget Pluto, which I own lock, stock, and barrel, and now I'm only one step from total control. Why it would be the same as giving up my life. Before I joined the Movement and became one of its leaders, I was nothing but a poor femfist living in a roach-infested room in Greenwich Village. I worked with my hands—look at them—gnarled and claw-like. I used to grow organic vegetables and peddle them on a cart through the Lower East Side. Sure, I'm a peasant. I'm proud of it."

"You should be, Chief. You're one of the great De-plorables."

"Well, you know what it's like, Furius. You've been there."

"And how! I got the Jersey ears to prove it."

"It's been a long hard struggle."

"But we've made it."

"Right, and ain't nobody goin' to take it away from us, unless it's over our dead bodies."

"Ya know, Chief, in a way, we're what made Atalanta great."

"A typical Atalanta success story, that's us. Gimme another shot, Furius."

"Coming up, Chief."

6

THE FUNDAMENTAL THINGS SURVIVE

I do not wish women to have power
over men; but over themselves.
                    —Mary Wollstonecraft

At midnight came a soft knock on the door of the corset room, and then a key was turned in the lock. Miz Mandalay, who had been dozing off, woke with a heart-stopping start, and sat up straight as her curves would allow.

"Who's there?" she cried.

"Shhh! It's Resurgius. May I come in and talk with you?"

"I don't suppose I can stop you," said Miz Mandalay, pulling several corsets up to cover her bare knobs. It was quite hot in the little room, so she was sleeping au naturel.

"Of course you can—if you wish," replied Resurgius, through the crack of the door; "but I wish you wouldn't. I've brought you some news."

"Very well then, enter. What news do you bring?"

"Sad news, but inevitable, I'm afraid," said Resurgius, coming in and closing the door behind him. "May I sit next to you?"

"Come ahead."

170

Resurgius seated his plastic muscle-bound self on a stack of panty girdles and adjusted his cape and hornrims. "It is a sad day," he said, "but a day that had to come. Edgahoova has declared war."

"What did I tell you? My kidnapping, far from doing you any good, has only given Edgahoova the chance she was looking for, not that she wouldn't have made one up anyway. But now she can get rid of me into the bargain. My doom has come, I see."

"Oh no; don't think that. I'll see to it that you come to no harm."

"You? But why should you?"

"I like you."

"You like me? I—your enemy?"

"Alas, I do. You are curve-bound as I am muscle-bound. Besides, what good would it do now to harm you? I'll simply hold you until the hostilities end."

"You're a strange Dong, Resurgius. I should think that you would hate me and my kind for what we've done to you. You described your life to me earlier, and I did feel sympathy for you. Shame-school must have been a terrible experience for a young Dong of pride, like you. You know, I have been working to abolish Shame-school, or at least modify it down to modesty."

"You would have been a fool to have done so. It's always been the most valuable weapon that the Mize have had. Without it, Dongs would have asserted themselves long ago."

"That's what Edgahoova always said."

"Edgahoova's is a cruel, greedy, and warped personality, but she has a brilliant political mind. She has never allowed herself to become confused in her motives. She wants power. She was an Alinsky radical before the Succession, a leading revolutionary through it, and, once

171

possessed of power, she became the extremist conservative in the Universe. That's how you get power and that's how you keep it. It's called triangulation."

"You make it sound like she never had an ideal. I think when she started out she wanted to do good," said Miz Mandalay.

"Yes, that's how we all rationalize our compulsion to control."

"Are you like that?"

"Probably, though I don't like to think so."

"Then why don't you desist?"

"Because we humans live in fear and search for power to control our little time while here. Death compels the search for power. It's natural not to."

"I would resist the compulsion to control, if I were in love."

"That's because you were born into everything on the up side. You'll find your true hunger in the descent," said Resurgius, shaking his head sadly.

"Pooh!"

"Kiss me."

"No."

"Why not?"

"No."

"Wouldn't you call in a Dong if you had the craves?"

"Yes . . ."

"Well?"

"But that's different. I don't know them."

"And do you know me?"

"Yes—a little."

"Not enough to say no. Don't you have the craves?"

"A little."

"Well then?"

"Well."

"There."

"Ooom!"

"Ah!"

"Oh!"

"Yi!"

"Mmm?"

"A-ha!"

"Wooo!"

"Weee!"

"Now then," said Resurgius, panting, afterward, "that wasn't so bad, was it?"

"Mmm!" purred Miz Mandalay. "You're a super Dong."

"Thanks, but I'd rather have you say you liked the real me, the skinny guy inside this parti-colored plastic muscle suit."

"Wasn't that the real you, Resurgius?"

"Shucks," said Resurgius, "you know what I mean. Say, do you believe in love at first see?"

"Absolutely not."

"Oh, I was afraid you'd say that."

"I thought you said you loved Miz Bet."

"Well, I do—or thought I did. I like her. She has those wonder-curves ever since the operation, but yours are better. You know, I've been thinking about what you said on the roof—that I was confusing love, sex, and gratitude? Maybe there's something in that."

"And now I suppose you think that you're in love with me. Just like a Dong! Indecently romantic."

"But suppose I am?"

"It's nothing to me if you are. You're beginning to upset me, Resurgius. If you think that this little super frisk is going to turn me into one of your dumb Cunnies, you're

173

mistaken. I'm a free Miz, with a life of my own. I don't do dishes or babies."

"Ah—but you're my prisoner—now. A prisoner of love!"

"Enough!" She waved him away. "This is what happens when one lets one's emotions get loose. I thank you for the excellent professional services that you've rendered me tonight. Now begone! I need my soma-coma."

"How hard and cold you grow!"

"How hard and hot you were! And how presumptuous you've become because of it! An inflatable plastic penis isn't everything—even when it's red, white, and blue. Please leave me, *Dong*!"

Resurgius went to the door; stopped and looked back at the raw hourglass lovely Miz Mandalay, her gorgeous sands flowing upward in the moonlight from the window, her ultra violets not cold, but somehow hurt and angry, as if in an instant they might fill with molten tears.

"Goodnight—Sweetheart," he said. "I think I love you." And he was gone.

The tears flew from Miz Mandalay's eyes, like the hot sparks of a welder, while she sat and called herself a fool. What kind of fool she wasn't sure.

"What kind of fool am I?" she asked the night. A fool for love, answered a leaden star.

7

ANABASIS

The next morning, Tuesday, Mae 14, 3000, Resurgius woke to news that the Shrike-Troopers, with the assistance of the Tactical Shrike-Police, were arresting and placing into Detention Camps all Dongs who were so unfortunate as to not have gone into hiding.

The roundup was being shown on Say-screen, and to watch it angered him.

Beth, filling Resurgius' bowl for the third time with vitamin-rich Vegan CoCo-Puffies, felt that the moment was propitious. "Strike now," she whispered into his crimson shell-like ear, "before they've arrested all those who would support you."

"You are right," said Resurgius, "this is no time for equivocation. The tide is at the flood. Let it lead on to fortune."

So saying, he contacted all his generals on a secret Me-pad channel; and ordering those whose headquarters were nearest the infamous Pinafore, headquarters for Furius and her Chiefs of Staff—three sisters named Claudia, Cossina, and Publia, who in pre-Succession days had been the singing group, French Kiss, and who now were suffering the pangs of the Change—to mount an offensive against that seat of war, hatred, and cattiness. Those of his generals whose headquarters were nearest the Detention Camps should set out to free the suffering, imprisoned Dongs. He himself would march on Martha, D.C.; his goal—take the Pink House and capture Jaye Edgahoova.

"But first, eat your Puffies," said Beth, and Resurgius took her hand affectionately and kissed it. She was always concerned to keep him erect and robust.

Within hours, Resurgius and a thousand of his cracked Yellow Berets were on the march, along the LaMer Turnpike.

Resurgius was exhilarated, now that he was in action, filled with the old gay combative spirit of his gladiatorial days on Say-screen. Now all he desired was a chance to smite and smote the enemy. But he had one regret, that circumstances had prevented him from saying farewell to Miz Mandalay, that curvy-wurvy darling. He had never before held in the palm of his hand a behind so soft as hers, and, nobody, not even the rain, had such small hands (he had recently visited the underground museum at Patchen Place). The trouble was, Beth watched him like a hawk, and if he had gone to say goodbye to Miz Mandalay, Beth would have suspected his attraction. Besides, the little darling was probably sleeping late—after last night, he added mentally, with a touch of vanity.

He was thinking of such things as these when one of his officers who had been scouting ahead came jogging down the road, crying that a large force of Tactical Shrike-Police were charging down the carmac to meet the Dongs. Even now, he was warned, they were halfway across Pankhurst Bridge, their lace collars like answers, blowing in the wind.

Knowing that this first engagement of the war would set the psychological standard for his Dongs, most of whom, because of their years at Shame-school, were a bit too hang-dong anyhow, he decided on an outrageous head-on attack, feet first, tooth and nail.

He calculated this way: his Yellow Berets outnumbered the force of Shrike-Police, and if he could make good time he could still meet those formidable sisters, Claudia, Cosina, and Publia, while they were on the bridge. That way they could not range themselves against him with more than, say, twenty abosom. If he had, as he calculated, roughly twice their number, he could let rank after rank, of both his and theirs, hack each other to pieces, and with their last rank up, and then done for, he would still have half his army, and the way across Pankhurst Bridge, his first great obstacle, should have been cleared.

"Brilliant strategy," his officers concurred, and busily arranged the Yellow Berets into ranks of twenty. When this was done, Resurgius ordered his Moog player to sound the charge, "I'm in the Moog for a Billingsgate Rumpus!"

Onward, along the LaMer Turnpike, at double-time, ray-guns at high port, rockets to the left of them, rockets to the right of them, charged the six hundred. Resurgius lead them, his bronzed pectoral muscles bouncing, his shapely calves knotting, his gold-and-flame hair like the beacon torch of the old Statue of Liberty, his great hornrimmed specks bouncing on his nose, and his hearty cry of "Hi-ho, Dongs!" ringing back over the heads of the Yellow Berets like a call to mad inspiration.

The Battle of Pankhurst Bridge, the first engagement of the war that would become known to the historians of future centuries as The Battle of the Sexes, had begun.

All happened as Resurgius had calculated. The Yellow Berets caught the Tactical Shrike-Police when they were a little more than half way across the bridge, and those survivors who were later to tell of their experience on that day, have oft been quoted as saying that the sound of the clash of the opposing forces could be likened to a recording of an old Hubert Humphrey speech being played backwards.

After raying down thirty Shrikes, Resurgius' pistol was emptied of sunbeams, and, throwing it into the big open mouth of a particularly grizzly adversary, thus strangling her last hurrah, he drew his broadsword, and, wielding it so that it seemed to acquire the blurring speed of rotation of an old-fashioned helicopter, sliced his way to the opposite end of the bridge, and, coming from the rear, repeated this action. Up and down the files of Tactical Shrike-Police Resurgius went, like a white tornado, slicing them like liverwurst, making minced meat of multitudes, until the stagnant waters of the River Slime turned red beneath the bridge with the blood of the Tactical Shrike-Police. It was a complete rout.

The Victorias were done for. The Victors could camp and have a party.

And when word of what had happened at Pankhurst Bridge reached Edgahoova, she summoned an Emergency meeting of Furius' Joint Chiefs and demanded an explanation of this disgraceful female failure.

"That force of Tactical Shrike-Police was caught napping, like sleeping beauties," said Edgahoova, her face aflame.

"You need a Pink Dongly, Chief?" asked Furius, concerned for her boss' health. "Or maybe a bit of distractive erotic zooaphilia; five minutes with Bob the Hog or maybe Sue the Sow?"

"Not now!" Edgahoova shouted back. "I'm too busy for craves! At a time like this Bob the Hog would just be boring."

Well, Chief," said Furius, "the Tactical Shrike-Police were just on a routine patrol. How could they know that Resurgius' Yellow Berets were on the LaMer Turnpike?"

"Balls! They know we're in a state of war, don't they? Now listen, I want no more such catastrophes! Aren't we all on Top Bulletin Alert? Send Claudia with a large army to search out Resurgius and to destroy him! Break through that plastic suit of his and get to the little worm inside!"

"Will do, Chief!" said Furius enthusiastically. "Government is fun, just like the old Mafia."

"I'll take that Pink Dongly now," Edgahoova said, wiping her brow and breathing more easily.

"But, Chief," said the wounded and bandaged Claudia, ignoring Furius, who was mixing a Dongly for the Chief, "did you know that the Pinafore is under siege? How can I leave it to go out in the field again looking for Resurgius?"

"Balls! You just don't wanna leave that cushy office of yours and that cute aide-de-camp you've got. Put Cossina in charge of the Pinafore siege resistance. You're the ablest commander I've got. I need you in the field."

And thus it was decided that Claudia would take an army and go to seek out Resurgius and engage him in mortal combat.

The position of the main Dong army was vaguely known at this time to be somewhere in the squeeze-box area of the Pocono Mountains, and so Claudia led her army in that direction. It was hard to tell because nobody had paid the satellite bill and the satellites had all wobbled out of position, blurring human intelligence.

At eleven o'clock, Wednesday morning, Mae 15, 3000, Claudia's point-scout reported sighting the point-scout of Resurgius' Yellow Berets. He did not see her, she said. This was exactly the kind of situation that Claudia was hoping for. Her Shrikes, refreshed with cocaine, greatly outnumbered Resurgius' Milltowned Dongs, and she also had the element of surprise working in her favor. Resurgius' troops were marching through a canyon of medium size, with steep escarpments to their right and left. They couldn't be more than twenty abreast. It was Pankhurst Bridge all over again, only this time the Shrike-Troopers had the advantages which Resurgius had had at the previous battle, those of number and surprise. Claudia was always ready to learn, even from a Dong. She decided that she would employ Resurgius' own tactic against him, and attack head on. She signaled her Moog player to sound the charge.

Unfortunately for Claudia's plan, however, Resurgius' point-scout, Tonto, had spotted Claudia's point, and returned to tell Resurgius that an army was moving against him. Making lightning calculations, Resurgius saw that he was in the same peril which the Tactical Shrike-Police had been in on Pankhurst Bridge, and reasoning that Claudia would charge, decided to avoid the encounter, which could only cause his army to suffer the same fate as that of the Tactical Shrike-Police.

Obviously, retreat was necessary. But retreat to where? He could never back his army up out of the canyon in time, with its sheer escarpments upward to either side. And he heard with deep concern the distant whine and cacophony of a Moog sounding the charge!

What to do?

Then he remembered the five backs of the Five Faces.

The Five Faces were stone portraits of five famous females which had been carved out of the gigantic rock-face of one of the major peaks of the Pocono Mountains by the famous Pip artist, Andrea Warlock. Not to be outdone by Mt. Rushmore's original monumentality, which had been made vague by winds and the sands of time, Warlock had one-upped the famous stone chipper, Borglum.

About a quarter of a mile back, Resurgius had passed an area which might have been climbed without too much difficulty, and had asked one of his Dongs if he knew where

180

it led. The Yellow Beret had answered that that area had been made accessible by engineers so that Andrea Warlock and her aides could climb up to chip at the Five Faces.

"That area," said the Dong, "would be the tushes, as it were, of the famous females whose faces are there."

"I'd like to see them," said Resurgius, with a twinkle in his eye.

They face off in the opposite direction," the Dong continued, "toward the Pink House.

"What," said Resurgius, "their behinds?"

"No, their tits. You have to climb up quite a distance to get to them, but you couldn't see anything, because of the bosom extension, unless you were to lower yourself down the front on a rope."

"Is it a long way down—and out—if you go over their foreheads?" asked Resurgius.

"Oh yes, a thousand feet, at least," his Dong answered. Resurgius now calculated the risks. It was either a matter of climbing to the summit of the Five Faces, and perhaps being trapped, or of attempting a hopeless retreat down the backs and asses, out of the canyon. He daringly opted for the Five Faces, and gave the order.

Fortunately for Resurgius, before the Shrike-Troopers under Claudia had entered the canyon, Resurgius' Dongs were within sight of the hackles of the statues. True, they were trapped, cornered, with no apparent way out, except back down over the big asses, a thousand feet into the canyon, where Claudia's huge force could easily annihilate them; but on the other hand, they were still intact, and Claudia would not dare to attack uphill, which is to say up the backs of the great women of the monument.

Resurgius' greatest fear, however, proved to be a likelihood. It was that Claudia, who was famous as a philistine, with an absolute detestation of art—and a personal grudge against Andrea Warlock, whom she had tried unsuccessfully to seduce at a Martha, D.C., political shindig—would call for a Rockcrusher missile to be brought to bear against his position.

Of course, he was right.

When Claudia entered the canyon, and saw what means Resurgius had used to make his escape, she did precisely that.

"We've got the Dongs trapped up there. They are impotent," she told her pretty aide-de-camp, whom she had decided to bring along, "call the Pinafore and tell my sister Cossina to sight in on the Five Faces with a Rockcrusher. While we're waiting for the fireworks we can have a picinicium."

But Resurgius had guessed as much, and even now behind his giant hornrims was bringing to bear all his powers of invention and analysis, to find a solution to his predicament.

He called for the Dong who had earlier told him about the statues and asked him:

"What, precisely, is their hair made of?"

"Well, as you know," the Dong answered, "Andrea Warlock is a Pip artist, famed for doing the unusual."

"Just answer the question," said Resurgius, "I'm not anymore interested in art, at this moment, than Claudia is."

"Yes, sir," said the Dong. "Well, the hair of the statues is made of kudzu vine, but in the case of Gloria Steinem, weeping willow, so that it actually grows, and has to be cut and re-coiffed every month or so. The State employs a large staff of gardener Mize who also are licensed beauticians to care for the upkeep. That's a particularly attractive *croquignole* wave that they've given Susan B. Anthony, don't you think?"

"Yeah, it's very attractive; but how long do you suppose it's been since they've had a trim?"

"Oh, I'd say they were about due."

"Then their hair is at its longest?"

"Mmm. Yes, I should say so."

"And how long would a hairdo like that, these *croquignole* waves, be if it were undone and combed down over Susan B. Anthony's face? Would it reach her knobs?"

"I should think it would reach down to her belly button."

"And if you had some of it cut and attached to the end of that?"

"To her knees."

"And—"

"Yes, I see your point."

"Then get busy with those shears. We're going down."

Resurgius' plan was a brilliant piece of cosmetological invention under pressure, but it wouldn't have worked if it hadn't been for the fact that no one at the Pinafore wanted to go along with Claudia and blow the statues to hell. The O.K. finally came, but it came too late.

By the time Cossina, back at the Pinafore, got word to go ahead, that Edgahoova herself had overruled all who were opposed, Resurgius' Yellow Berets were already sliding and kicking their way down the noses of the five faces.

There they were—Susan B. Anthony, Margaret Sanger, Eleanor Roosevelt, Betty Freidan, and Gloria Steinem—with their kudzu and weeping willow streaming down over their faces, and Resurgius' Yellow Berets sliding down the strands right over their enormous titties. Resurgius was the first over a forehead. Dauntless, he slid down one of Betty Freidan's hairs, winking as he lowered himself past her left eye, and was the first to touch the ground.

Soon, all but one of the Yellow Berets were down. He had stayed behind in order to throw the ray guns down to his military comrades. Unfortunately, this brave trooper was killed in the blast that followed; he would later be honored at special ceremonies, at what was to become the tomb of the Unknown Dong.

Reaching the ground, Resurgius regrouped his Yellow Berets, marched around the Pocono Mountains, and, entering the canyon by both mouths, surprised that picnicking and cavorting army of Claudia's, achieving his second victory of the Sex War, which was to be known as the Battle of the Five Faces. By the time the mountain was blown up, his troopers were already chasing many of the surviving and now unarmed Shrike-Troopers into the bushes. The success of the Yellow Berets in these sub-skirmishes must have been great, for many of the Shrike-Troopers, stout and nimble Mize, revolted over to the Dongs' side and became traitors, surrendering to slobbering love. Resurgius returned their weapons to some of them, who joined the ranks of his best shocking troops, while others, of somewhat questionable sincerity, he allowed to become scouts, like the great Tonto.

Unfortunately, Claudia, who had been bathing in a nearby tributary of the River Slime, made her escape by running along the bed of that river with a twenty foot hollow reed in her mouth. She emerged, stark naked and covered with leeches, three miles from the scene of battle. However, Resurgius had succeeded in capturing her luggage, which consisted of five hundred assorted suitcases and hat boxes.

But, even though she had temporarily made her escape, Claudia's fate was sealed.

Early Thursday morning, Mae 16, 3000, Resurgius' advance guard caught up with her at the Appomattox Public Baths, where she had retired in order to rid herself of the leeches. A few hours later, she handed her hollow reed to

Resurgius and retired from the war in disgrace. Thus ended the public career of a great Soldress, who, alas, had made the mistake of calling down a Rockcrusher upon the images of five heroines of her own revolution. It is an ironic footnote to history, that today she is a quiet-living, unassuming grandmother, the wife of a village blacksmith.

Entre nous, Edgahoova was pleased at the idea of blowing up the Five Faces. More room for her big head.

8

KATABASIS

Plus ça change,
plus c'est la même chose.
—*Jean-Baptiste Alphonse Karr*

At this point in the war Resurgius began to experience his first difficulties with his own Dongs. They, alas, grown confident in their numbers, and erected with their successes, began to break away in small groups by night to go about ravaging the suburbs of Atalanta. Thus was it ever, that achieved power in a common goal will immediately lead to division among the powerful. For, one of the ironies of human life is, to be anything, one must be oneself, and to be oneself one must assert against others, for the line between the self and others can only consist of such an assertion— the hacking warrior and the catatonic guru are employed in the same pursuit.

So now Edgahoova's position became visibly strengthened with outraged pubic opinion, and Resurgius, who had staked so much on the hope of making converts, found that much of the countryside had turned against him—disruption and war annoyed most people, for they had personal lives. And to add to his burdens, a group of his Dongs now suffered a severe defeat. To be sure, it was only a small group, and in no way representative of his main force, yet this first victory of the Shrike-Troopers had a demoralizing impact on the Dongs.

It seemed that Edgahoova, upon receiving word of Claudia's defeat and capitulation, had ordered Claudia's sister Cossina, who had sung bass, out into the field, and her first day out, with beginner's luck, she had fallen suddenly upon a party of Dongs, who through contempt and confidence had straggled away from the main body of Resurgius' troops, and so she had hacked the careless Dongs to chipped beef. It was an easy victory, for the Dongs were over-laden with portable Say-screens which they had pillaged from the window of a local Amazon Mart. But, nonetheless, the victory had the effect of raising the morale of the Shrikes and lowering that of the Dongs.

However, this reversal was only temporary; for Resurgius, realizing that something must be done to recoup his loss, the major importance of which was moral, not military, counter-attacked, and, joining in battle, defeated Cossina's chief officers, and captured all of Cossina's own baggage—one thousand assorted suitcases, hatboxes and shoe racks—Cossina herself making a hairsbreadth escape.

When Edgahoova heard of this, she was fit to be tied, and in a double ceremony, though in absentia, she had Claudia and Cossina drummed out of the army. No one claimed that this was jealousy. Upon getting word of her status, Cossina, enraged at having dishonor heaped upon her head by Edgahoova, defected to Resurgius, and was placed in charge of the army that was then laying siege to the Pinafore. With Publia now in charge at that venerable seat of infamy, the war had added to all its other ironies that of pitting sister against sister.

When Edgahoova saw the unpleasant turn things were taking, she decided to play her trump card, and put the ear-biting Furius herself in command of the most massive army ever assembled by Atalanta. It was not too difficult to put such an army together, for now a great many of the nobility—that is, those who owned one or more states—about sixty families—volunteered to help suppress the underdog Dongs, partly out of friendship for Edgahoova, whose cause of using the unlanded little people as a labor force to produce wealth on the land they owned, they were in complete sympathy with, and partly to gain honor.

There was anger among the Deplorables at being disrupted. In the streets they were given to singing rebellious songs, like "Curious Furius, She's a Dong," and carrying placards like the following:

The Vanderhorns own most of Arkanstate,
the Heebeejeebeezes own Kent;
a few score others own the rest of Freedom,
and we, the people, pay the rent.

Furius, a canny warrior, instead of marching to the attack, as Claudia and Cossina had done, stayed with the main body of her army on the border of Martha, D.C., expecting that Resurgius would come that way, and sent her lieutenant, Mammius, with two legions of Tactical Shrike-Police, to wheel about and observe the enemy's motions, but upon no account to engage or skirmish. But Mammius, upon the first opportunity, joined battle, and was routed, having a great many of her Shrikes slain, and a great many only saving their lives with the loss of their weapons. Furius rebuked Mammius severely, biting off one of her ears; and, arming the Shrikes once more, she made them give sureties for their new weapons, that they'd not part with them again; and five-hundred that were the beginners of the fight, she divided into fifty tens, and one of each, by lot, she bit the ears from, before the eyes of the whole army, assembled as spectators, to prove her power.

When she had thus disciplined her Shrikes, she led them out against the enemy. But now, Resurgius, seeing that he would be overwhelmed, retreated up the River Slime, with Furius in hot pursuit. Indeed, by Friday morning, Mae 15, 3000, Furius had begun to overtake Resurgius.

And so, Resurgius made a serious gamble, and avoiding the Pocono Mountains, turned his weary force in the direction of the nearest Spaceport.

Now during these trying times Spaceports were occupied by tremendous bands of Space-Pirates. They had complete operational control of most Spaceports, and a special branch of the government had been set up, by the year 2050, to pay them an official danegeld in order to assure safe and efficient space travel. The Air-Traffic-Controlling Pirates ran the Spaceports admirably, but they demanded complete freedom from government interference, and since they could in no wise be controlled or suppressed, without extended, expensive conflicts, government had found it expedient to grant them immunity and give them semi-official recognition. They became known as the A.S.P.s or Atalantan Space-Pirates, and their right of legal exemption from the laws of Atalanta was approved by a long succession of governments, proving once again, for the as yet unconvinced, that, in politics at least, might makes right.

In any case, these Space-Pirates and their Spaceports were untouchable, and no force of the government's would dare to march upon them, for, if they did, Space travel would be hopelessly snarled; and out of this had come the tradition of using Spaceports very much as churches had been used during the Dark Ages, as places of sanctuary. If the Space-Pirates were in sympathy with your cause, they might take you in—but they'd be much more likely to take you in if you could pay them some form of danegeld, like cigarettes (a valuable artifact), or any kind of booze or drugs. An added source of hope for Resurgius was the fact that these pirates had no particular political affiliation, having seen clear through politics to its twin points of reference, money and power, and having decided to skip the bull shit rhetoric. They were comprised of all four sexes, and did little else but eat, drink, drug and fornicate in some amazing combos like drugged monkeys.

It was on the evening of Friday, Mae 17, 3000, that Resurgius and his weary Dongs entered the main gate of the Wanda Von Braunkirk Spacecenter and Port; and, surprisingly, to a hero's welcome. The Space-Pirates had been following the blazing course of the war on Say-screen; and, Edgahoova, recently having vetoed a bill to increase their tribute, for which they had spent a great deal of time and, worse, money, lobbying—having paid out a total of twenty-billion Bit Coins in bribes to officials—they had been on the verge of causing a total snarl in Space-traffic, when the war had broken out, and naturally were very sympathetic to Resurgius; of course, they also saw the possibility of a deal.

In one of the world's great backroom deals, Resurgius, too, saw this possibility. In fact, the deal would be his tribute.

After the formalities of the first meeting, the leaders retired to the control tower for a private session, leaving Resurgius' Dongs and Shrike defectors to get acquainted with their counterparts among the Space-Pirates. Within minutes these had undertaken a marvelous bacchanal, so that for a thousand yards there was nothing to be seen but a hideously squirming daisy-chain, consisting of twenty thousand naked simian bodies.

Meanwhile, the leaders sat down before plates of assorted happy pills, including dream heaps of little red diablos, and began their conference. The main spokesman for the Space-Pirates was one Blackbeard, a Miz of robustious humor and keen mind.

"That was a marvelous and unexpected welcome," Resurgius began, feeling her up and out.

"A show of unity with your cause, my dear Resurgius," said Blackbeard, popping down several little red diablos. "We Space-Pirates think very highly of you."

"And of my cause?"

"Which is?"

"Freedom, égalité, et fraternité—or if you would prefer, sororité."

"As a woman," said Blackbeard, "I see it as a fine and noble cause, but before you can achieve such high ideals you must seize power. Many heads must roll! There must be one of those new electronic guillotines brought to the pubic square!"

"It's true," said Resurgius, "that only through my accession to supreme power can the Universe hope to see again what you might call the just life. Alas, the burden of leadership weighs heavily upon my extremely broad shoulders."

"Take care, Resurgius, that it doesn't weigh down those plastic shoulders of yours."

"I suppose that you are making reference to the fact that I am in military retreat."

"You must admit," said Blackbeard, with her super red Revloned lips in a guileful smile that tilted her black beard, "that it weakens your position. Immediately after the Battle of the Five Faces—incidentally, a brilliant piece of work—"

"Thanks."

"—we had begun to conceive of a plan whereby we might throw our considerable power in your direction, if—"

"Of course. I understand your position with regard to Martha, D.C., and Edgahoova."

"Yes, I knew that you'd understand. But now—here you are in full retreat. Things don't look very hopeful."

"You paint too black a picture, Blackbeard. Let's speak plainly. You are only trying to drive up your price for supporting me."

"Well, let's face it, Resurgius, the odds have altered, our gamble is a much greater one now. And let me remind you, that at this moment, we Space-Pirates are the only force standing between you and Furius."

"Yet you've seen that I'm resourceful, and might come up with a ploy that could alter everything again, and wind me into supreme power."

"Well, that is why we have welcomed you. We know that you've been in bad situations before and have survived to conquer. But still, we'd be taking a big gamble to support you. You desired that we should speak plainly. Very well, what is our support worth to you?"

"Fair question, Blackbeard. I propose to offer you, if I am successful, all the states now owned and operated by Edgahoova, to the number of three, with a labor population totaling three-hundred million. The revenues from the natural resources and industries alone should come to something in the neighborhood of twenty trillion ultra bobbits—the big green—every year, and all social services—schools, hospitals, etc.—are completely paid for out of the pockets of the working middle-class, who also support the poor through taxation, which will leave your revenue to be a clear profit, just as it is for Edgahoova now. What say you to that? Is that a deal or what?"

"What about a counter-proposal?"

"Go ahead."

"How about, in addition to those states owned by Edgahoova, throwing in those owned by Miz Mandalay, Furius, Cossina, Publia, Claudia and Miz Bet."

"Miz Bet only owns one state, through her mother, and I intend to keep that. After all, Miz Bet is my wife."

"What about the others?"

"Well, you must be able to see that I'll have to have some states to give to my Dongs, especially my generals, and, as for Cossina's states, I'll have to let her keep them, now that she's come over to my side, else what would she be fighting for?"

"I thought she was fighting for freedom."

"Don't be snide. Of course she's fighting for freedom. She's fighting for the freedom to keep her states. Haven't you heard of incentive?"

And thus they wrangled on all night and into the early hours of dawn, when the only sounds aside from the wind in the wires and their own voices, was the last soft sequence of random orgasms from the field, the sipping of rum, and the hissing of pot.

Finally, at ten o'clock Saturday morning, Mae 18, 3000, they came to an agreement. In return for her services, Blackbeard was to get the following:

1. All those states owned by Edgahoova and Furius.

2. All those Spaceports which were not now controlled by the Space-Pirates turned over to them.

3. Resurgius' government would double the danegeld now being paid to the Space-Pirates.

4. All Offense plants were to be handed over to Blackbeard's first cousin, who was a banker, and would make a respectable front.

5. Resurgius would guarantee the continuation of the war on the Dark Side of the Moon, so that there would be a place to drop bombs and explode missiles in order to supply a reason to keep the Offense plants operating.

6. Resurgius would, naturally, agree to a higher Offense budget.

For her part, Blackbeard was prepared to offer full co-operation with Resurgius, and to prove her good faith, they sealed their bargain with a kiss. Resurgius wiped his mouth with the back of his hand, and Blackbeard applied fresh lipstick. It was a distasteful end to difficult negotiations.

9

THE GREAT WALL OF FURIUS

Meanwhile, Furius had not been idle. Only a short league behind the tail of Resurgius' army as it had entered the gates of the Wanda Von Braunkirk Spacecenter and Port, Furius had her army set up a camp while she contemplated the circumstances. To charge the Spacecenter was unthinkable. To call down a Grandsmasher upon it was out of the question, more especially in view of the sad fate of Claudia, who even now was pregnant with her first Accidental by the filthy village blacksmith with whom she had got drunk in order to console herself. In the midst of action she had forgotten to take her Defetus pills.

No, any kind of attack was out of the question. If the Space-Pirates had taken Resurgius in, they would fight for him, and their numbers were large. Cripes, hadn't she warned Edgahoova of the folly of vetoing that increase in their danegeld! Secretly she sometimes thought her Chief was a vain fool.

But then a plan began to hatch in her mind. And what a plan! If she could bring it off, not only would she have Resurgius trapped and save the Atalantan way of life, to which purpose she was officially sworn, but she could make herself a nice little bit coin boodle on the side.

She got into communication with the Pinafore, the gist of her message being this (later made public as part of the Pinafore Papers):

"Have Resurgius and his Dongs trapped at the Wanda Von Braunkirk Spacecenter. Attack out of the question. Recommendation: Complete entrapment. Method: the construction of a moat, canalizing sludge from the River Slime, and the construction, within the perimeter of the moat, of a gigantic wall, to be known as the Great Wall of Furius, hereinafter:

"Naturally, the public would object to the use of Tactical Shrike-Police or Shrike-Troopers for the purpose, so I suggest that you give my aunt, Jennifer Thickneck, of Wonder Woman Constructions, a contract for the work. Note: the following is to be classified Top Secret. It must be understood by Auntie Thickneck that I am to get fifty percent of the profits paid her by the taxpayers for this work in return for the contract. If this plan is acceptable to all, a percentage of my fifty percent will find its way back to all who approve. Naturally, my army will do the actual labor, as a service to the country."

Within minutes a bill had been passed by both Houses, whose members were reached at various resorts on The Sea of Tranquility; and, all agreeing on the matriotic importance of the work, the Shrike-Troopers were issued backhoes and began digging.

By Saturday morning, just as Resurgius and Blackbeard came to final terms, Furius laid the last plastic brick to the wall which would forever bear her name. This great and difficult work she perfected in a space of time short beyond all expectation, digging a ditch from the banks of the River Slime to the gates of the Wanda Von Braunkirk Spacecenter and on around the whole port. Within this roiling moat of sludge stood a gleaming wall of fine pink plastic bricks eighty feet high, with large ducts at its base to allow the River Slime in, and so drown those inside, and with Atalantan flags flying from every turret, which was twenty feet from its likeness to left and right.

Upon first sight of this great wall and the moat beyond it, Resurgius slighted and despised it as unimportant, but when he realized that provisions were short, he began to worry, as did Blackbeard, who was a Miz, as Resurgius had come to know, of hearty appetites. Soon there was great fear in the Spacecenter that they should all starve because of the wall; and it was that fear, and the hysteria that came in its wake, which led directly to what later historians have come to call The Day of Infamy, which was Sunday, Mae 19, 3000. At the same time, Resurgius, who was never neglectful of the need for military discipline, was drilling his Dongs in another part of the Spacecenter, and Blackbeard and her Space-Pirates, occupying all the available Rockettes, deserted him, taking off for the Moon.

10

ESCAPE FROM THE SPACEPORT

*Yet that things go round and again go round
Has rather a classical sound.*
                              —*Wallace Stevens*

Just as Resurgius discovered Blackbeard's infamous desertion of him, a great Spring deluge began to pelt the land and swell the River Slime, dilating its rather turgid water and sending it roaring with tremendous force over its bed of sludge. This in turn drove a great deal of water into the canal which Furius had dug, and, in a short time, caused the waters of the moat to rise perceptibly against the plastic brick of the Great Wall of Furius. And this fact gave Furius an idea that, giving the devil her due, must go down as one of the most brilliant military ploys in history; right beside the Trojan Horse, Custard's Stand, or the brilliant Ride of the Six Hundred.

"We'll drown 'em like rats!" she cried.

When asked by one of her lieutenants what her meaning was, she elaborated:

"That's my plan," she said, "That's what the ducts are for. Get it?"

"The Spacecenter will fill up like a bathtub!"

198

"Right," said Furius, "and we can attach pumps to make sure that it does. As soon as Resurgius and his motley crew of Dongs, Cunnies, Hookers, and Shrike-Groupies see that they're going to be drowned, they'll make for the exit, where we can pick them off one by one as they come out. They'll have to leave before the water can get deep enough to do any lasting damage to the Spaceport, so nobody can ever blame me for destroying it, the way they blamed Claudia for destroying the Five Faces Univacual Monument, and I'll issue strict orders not to shoot any of the Space-Pirates, and that way we can avoid a Space snarl. How does it sound?" (It should be noted here that Furius was unaware of the escape of the Space-Pirates, for at the time of their departure she was in her mobile command post, exercising her hobby, pickling and jarring ears.)

"It sounds brilliant," said her lieutenant, "should I issue the orders?"

"Yes, and *vaya con Dios*, my darling. If my plan works, we'll have a victory celebration in the form of a Matronalia as soon as the weather clears, and I don't mean an old fashioned Matronalia, I mean a panting-mouth and erected-tongue Matronalia! Hot damn!"

"Oh, goodie!" cried the lieutenant. "I just love a good Matronalia." And she went off to give the orders. Within hours the cry went up inside the Spaceport that the place was filling with water. Already now it was up to the average Dong's knees, and was rising rapidly.

"We'll all be drowned!" cried the more hysterical among the entrapped.

"Let's make a break for it out the front gates," cried the intrepid in unison.

"They'll mow us down as we come out," cried the timorous, "let's surrender instead."

It was at this point that Resurgius took action. Speaking in a firm stage-whisper over a loud speaker from the control tower, he gathered the attention of the disputants and forced them to apply reason to the crisis, saying:

"It is true that we have been deserted by our former ally, Blackbeard, and her Space-Pirates, and that we now must face the fact that we all may be drowned. It is also true that if we attempt to make our escape by wading or swimming out the main gate, which Furius has left to be the only exit in her diabolical wall, for there is no lock on it, and it opens outward, then we will all be killed; for surely she awaits without it, and she has vowed to take no prisoners"— this was not true, but Resurgius thought it might encourage his Dongs to consider a plan which he'd been hatching— "and isn't it plain to all of you that she wants us to leave by that gate, and that that is why she is flooding the Spaceport? If we go out that gate—either fighting or in surrender—we are done for. Now think on this:

"There are three elements which accommodate the traveller—land, air, and water. We cannot go by land, for there is an unscalable wall around us and an army in waiting outside its only exit. We cannot go by air, for our quondam allies, the Space-Pirates, have taken every craft that flies. Now, my ingenious Dongs, let me hear *you* solve the problem of your escape!"

From the knee-deep Dongs there arose a tremendous shout of "Water! We shall escape by water!"

"Exactly!"

"But how?" they cried.

In answer, Resurgius extended a bronzed and muscled arm and pointed at the administration building, across the way from him. It was a huge, zebra-striped, plastic edifice which had been modeled on the classic lines of the Ancient

Pan-Am Building, which had once stood, albeit a little drunkenly, in the heart of Old Manhattan.

"Eureka!" he cried, his voice a dramatic and prophetic kettle-drum behind the incessant *Mama-poppa*! *Mama-poppa*! of the rain. "There is your answer! 'Make thee an ark of gopherwood!' But we have no need for gopherwood, when we have a completely pre-fab plastic ark at our disposal. That thing'll float! All we have to do is to unmoor it, by which I mean throw all those computers out of it, and detach it from its foundations. It'll hold every last Dong of you. It'll be the Ark of the Deplorable Dongs! Get busy!"

Soon the Administration Building was afloat, and in a formal ceremony in the penthouse Resurgius was made an Admirable. "As surely as the water rises, we shall rise and sing," he had proclaimed, and sure enough they did. But it was a slow process, for it took billions of tons of water to fill the Spaceport and to float Resurgius' ark to the top of the wall. The new-fledged Admirable stood at his post in the penthouse all night as his fifty-story ship rose toward the stars rocking and swaying and creaking like an old tug at anchor.

Soon, though, the penthouse cleared the top of the wall, and Resurgius could look out over Furius' camp. Sure enough, a great body of troops was gathered at the gate, waiting for the Dongs to come out, and half drowning themselves in the waterfall deluge.

The whole countryside, as well, was under a greater siege than either Dong or Shrike could create: the siege of weather. In fact, Resurgius laughed to think, his troops were probably a lot dryer than those of Furius. Indeed, the whole countryside was melting into mud, and spattering back upon itself.

Perhaps it was this very feminine softness of the earth that reminded Resurgius of Miz Mandalay—or as he had come to think of her; Mandy—and of the softness of her behind. Oh, that he might be back at the brassiere factory right now, and have a few moments in the corset room with her!

And as it so happened, Miz Mandalay was at that very moment thinking thoughts analogous to his.

She had been able to follow the whole course of the war on Say-screen; and, at first, when Resurgius had been winning, had felt the strangest mixed feelings of her life. She felt a definite sensation of fear that he might win, which no doubt would alter her whole mode of life, and yet at the same time she could not help feeling a certain pride in his success, as though, somehow, it were her own.

"It's the craziest thing," she thought, "he's beating me at my own game and I seem to like it that he is. What could it mean?" Then, later, when he began to suffer reverses, instead of being matriotically glad, as indeed it was her duty to be, she actually became terrified for him. She even began trying to think how she might be able to save him. "It's all very unmatriotic of me," she thought, "but I can't help how I feel about that big golden ape."

And now, just having seen the Nightie Show, and being aware of his being trapped within the walls of the Spaceport, and with all that water rising up above his silver boots—well, she just couldn't help herself, and had fallen onto a stack of corsets, where she was presently engaged in crying her eyes, and heart, out.

"Oh, my poor Dong!" she wept. "All you wanted was to be treated like a person, and look what we've done to you—turned you into a fugitive, a hunted animal, an heroic rat! Oh, that you were only here in my arms, that I might comfort you! If you are fortunate enough to be saved, and to return to me, I'll never say those awful things I said to you again! And I'll love you love you love you," she added, panting.

And at that very moment the first floor of the Administrative Building rose even with the top of the Great Wall of Furius, and, turning and turning, like a rubber ducky caught in a maelstrom, it slid in the out gush of water over the wall and dropped, rocking, into the swirling moat, where it was immediately caught by the current and sent off at eighty miles an hour around the Spaceport.

Glancing up out of the window of her mobile command post, from her self-appointed task of sealing a jar of pickled ears, Furius saw the Administration Building go by on its first turn on the moat. Immediately, she went on Sayscreen to report that victory was hers.

"Even now," she told the public, "debris from inside the Spaceport can be seen travelling at great velocity atop the whirling waters, and there can be no doubt that all rebels inside the walls have been drowned. Victory is ours!"

Upon hearing a late report of which, Miz Mandalay became inconsolable, and tried to hang herself by a garter. She had to be shoved into six corsets to restrain her powerful Amazonian self.

Beth, on the other hand, debated with herself whether it wasn't time to get in touch with Jaye Edgahoova and claim that she'd been kidnapped. In order to get away with that, however, she would have to see to it that Miz Mandalay's next suicide attempt was successful.

But Beth was too clever to leap before she'd looked. She decided to wait time out, and see if it wasn't possible that Resurgius had escaped. This wasn't to be attributed to loyalty on her part, but to an instinct for survival. For, if he were alive, Resurgius could incriminate her; and he would have to be taken care of before she could go back over to Edgahoova's side.

"It's all very sad," she thought. "I really loved that Dong. Really I did. And I really despise old Edgahoova. But I guess she'll just have to do. If Resurgius' army is drowned, what good is he?" But, fortunately for her, her respect for Resurgius' resourcefulness was so strong that she waited to hear some more definite confirmation of his death. And that would never come: for Resurgius, now an Admirable, was very much alive, and in command of the floating Ark.

All night Resurgius' Ark circled the Spaceport and each time it got to the far side, where Furius could not see, fifty more of his Dongs leaped to the bank of the moat. By morning, he had regrouped his army on the other side of the Spaceport and was already drippingly on the march.

11

A MATRONALIA AND A MUTINY

Monday, Mae 20, 3000. The weather had cleared and the gay sun had come out of hiding, dancing everywhere in its golden slippers.

Furius, still believing Resurgius and all of his Dongs to have been drowned, gave her permission for the Matronalia to begin, and now it was in full swing. This Matronalia was nothing but a modern revision of the old pagan rite, which had generally been held on the first of March in ancient times, and which consisted of the counterpart to the Saturnalia, or male festival, wherein masters feasted their slaves, and exchanged places with them, allowing them to give the orders, and generally bully and make fun of their masters— in other words, a day of Misrule. In the Matronalia of pagan times the same was done, the mistresses feasting their slaves as masters did theirs at Saturnalia. Now, in the days after the Great Succession the Matronalia had been revised, though in a somewhat different form, and to be held at any time the circumstances seemed appropriate—for instance, right after an election, or, as here, on the successful completion of a mission or task.

This revision of the Matronalia was mainly the work of Sally Hurok, the great impresaria, who held the first Post-Succession Matronalia in Dolly Madison's Garden, to celebrate the success of the Succession. The Dongs, who were at that point completely enslaved (this was well before Abby Lincoln's Emancipation Proclamation of 1995) were allowed to mock and generally abuse the Mize present, who seemed to enjoy this turning of the tables immensely. Tootles and gay giggles rang out.

And so it was now, in Furius' camp.

The Dongs captured on the Martha Washington Bridge and other places, now prisoners of war, had been released from their cages for the occasion, and were busily employed in chasing giggling Shrike-Troopers. The Shrikes would run ahead, as in days of old, and the Dongs would run after them, stark naked, and holding their erected members in their hands, shouting such phrases as "Wait, my little chickadee," or, what many of the Shrike-Troopers preferred, "Stop, sexual object!" And then the Shrike-Troopers, also, of course, naked, would stop in their tracks, bend forward, and place their hands on their knees, and wait to be rammed. Such fun! Such gaiety! It made all forget the rigid ranking of the class system they lived under.

It was great sport, and everyone, including Furius, who had been rammed five times, was having a wonderful time. Furius had chosen as her partner for the Matronalia a particularly ugly old Dong who was toothless, but for a marvelously Dracula-like set of fangs, or dog-teeth, and was about to suggest to him that he might nibble on her ears, if he so desired, when a Highway Patrol Shrike came into camp, the bearer of bad tidings. It seemed that Resurgius and most of his army had survived, and were encamped not five miles distant.

If this was bad news for Furius, Resurgius himself had only minutes before he received equally bad news.

Only an hour earlier, two of Resurgius' more militant commanders, "Old Blood" Castratus and "Old Guts" Cunnilingus, had come blustering up to his command post, which was in a hollow tree, to complain that he had been misusing his army.

"We must attack," said Old Blood.

"Attack!" echoed Old Guts.

"But we can't attack," Resurgius objected. "They have us greatly outnumbered."

"We would have been in Martha, D.C., now, and eating slamburgs in the Pink House, if you hadn't started retreating. We think you're yellow! There!"

"Yellow!" echoed Old Guts.

"That's up to you," said Resurgius, coolly, eying them through his hornrims, "you may think what you will of me, but I'll not have my whole army chopped to pieces because of your hotheadedness. Once my little army of Yellow Berets is lost, the revolution itself is lost. We are in a Dunquirkian situation."

"But we haven't fought a good battle since the Five Faces," cried Old Blood. "All we do is retreat, like a bunch of sissy scaredy-cats."

"Sissy scaredy-cats!" Old Guts emphasized.

"You know perfectly well that I'm no sissy," said Resurgius, flushing. "Look at these muscles," he added, flexing his enormous powder-blue biceps. He removed his spectacular hornrims. "I am employing a time-honored tactic of military science, made famous by the great Roman General Fabius Maximus, when, in retreating, he caused his adversary, Hannibal, to overextend his lines of supply, and get way out in front of his skis."

"Bah!" cried Old Blood. "There's only one way to fight—attack, attack, attack! Rape! Pillage! Destroy! Blowup! Kill! Maim! Slaughter! Desecrate! Feet First, Tooth, and Nail! That's the only way to find peace in our time!"

"You have always disgusted me with your mixed metaphors," said Resurgius.

"Bah!" cried Old Guts. "Similes are better. Like, I like chaos and disorder. They're the fun of war." And the two generals stalked off cursing, hand in hand.

And, within the hour, Resurgius was brought news that Old Blood Castratus and Old Guts Cunnilingus had deserted camp, taking with them over a third of Resurgius' bravest Dongs.

"Well," he said, philosophically, "they're two of my best commanders; what good will it do to force them to stay? Perhaps they'll be able to harass Furius enough to allow me to make a getaway with my remaining Dongs. Still, I'd hate to see a third of my Dongs blown to bits." And so, he ordered that a scout go out after the mutineers and check as to their whereabouts, and see if they might need help.

It had been just as Old Blood and Old Guts left camp with a third of Resurgius' army, that a Highway Patrol Shrike, on routine duty, happened to spot them. Thinking that she might get a promotion to a cushy desk job, where she could indulge herself in her hobbies of listening to high-decibel screeching electronic music, or slap-happy rap that rhymed really good dirty words, if she were to bring this off, she carefully followed Old Blood and Old Guts to Lake Gunk, a kind of cul-de-crap, which is fed by the River Slime, where they made a separate camp. She had to laugh, knowing the area, for Lake Gunk was out of season, and she knew that the mutineers would be mighty thirsty before long. For the fact was, that Lake Gunk was a fine place to camp, and the water very drinkable, in late summer, when the waste matter from a local Cathy Cola factory was poured into it—at which time a chemical analysis would show that it was about fifty percent pure Cathy Cola, which was a very strong germicide—but now, in mid-Mae, it became almost ninety percent pure Dizzy Detergent, and acquired the consistency of chocolate pudding, and was completely undrinkable and smelly—which was a good reason for finishing her investigation in a hurry, before nostrilitus set in, and they were forced to move on to find some kind of potable liquid.

So, this clever Highway Patrol Shrike, looking forward to the days at hand when she would be able to sit all day and listen to electronic noise, retraced her steps and, by following the trail from which Old Blood and Old Guts had emerged, came upon Resurgius' camp.

Hurrying back to the Furius encampment, she reported, breathlessly, "There's a group of apparent Dongzerters camped on the banks of Lake Gunk, and Resurgius and his main body of troops are just a bit farther on."

"Stunk? Skunk?"

"Gunk," repeated the Highway Patrol Shrike.

"You mean to tell me that they're alive?" cried Furius, tugging her left ear free of the fanged mouth of the venerable old Dong. "Are you trying to tell me that I failed to destroy them? That they got away?"

"I'm afraid it's true," said the Highway Patrol Shrike, importantly. She couldn't wait to get her reward. But she became a little uncertain when she saw that Furius was turning purple with rage.

"You!" cried Furius suddenly. "You dare to bring me such rotten news!" With which, she pounced upon the poor Highway Patrol Shrike and bit off both her ears, which effectively ended the latter's enjoyment of electronic music, and earrings.

Furius' first thought, after pickling the Highway Patrol Shrike's ears, was that Resurgius might be planning to avoid contact with her army, so that he could make a straight run down to Martha, D.C., and seize the ottoman of power, in the Pink House. The more she thought about it, the more likely it seemed that he would do just that. Well, she thought, she could turn that to her own advantage. What she could do would be to let Resurgius avoid her and head south; then, using her F-phone, she would contact Publia at the Pinafore, and order her to place the Pinafore in some-body else's charge, and to bring an army up from Martha, D.C. That would put Resurgius between herself, in the North, and Publia, in the south; they would have him trapped. Post-hasty, she got in touch with Publia and ex-plained her plan. Publia agreed, and placed the Pinafore, which was still under siege by Resurgius' Southern army, the Dixiecrat Dongs, in the charge of an underling, and started on the march north.

"I'm not going to attack Resurgius' main body," said Furius, explaining her strategy to a group of her command-ers. "He's too slippery, and might get away. I'm going to wait until he makes his run for the South, which is what I'm certain he's going to do, and only when I have him trapped between Publia and us, will I attack. But I don't like the idea of letting those mutineer Dongs get clean away. Be-sides, I'm itching for a fight. And remember Fight makes Right. So I think I'll take a small contingent of Shrikes and go out to Lake Gunk and clean them up," she giggled, "or hose them down." She liked her own quip and, meaning to laugh, farted. "Any volunteers?"

Fifty Shrike-Troopers volunteered, and within the hour she came down upon the mutineer Dongs under the com-mand of Old Blood Castratus and Old Guts Cunnilingus and began to chase them from the banks of the Gunk; but she could not pursue the slaughter because Resurgius came sud-denly upon the scene and checked the fight. He had been told by the scout whom he had sent to follow Old Blood and Old Guts that they had also been followed by a Highway Patrol Shrike, and Resurgius had decided to go and check upon their safety—he arrived just in time, as historical fate would have it.

Now Furius was really furious. She returned to her camp, mustered her whole army, and set off to engage Resurgius, who by this time had left the mutineers' camp and returned to his own. He had tried once again to talk Old Blood and Old Guts into returning with him, but had failed. It was all very sad, for he saw his army, and with it his revolutionary hopes, falling apart with internal discord, like an upset stomach. Many of his Dongs felt blue and wanted only to make a run for their hideout at the brassiere factory; others, of a different temperament, inclined to agree with Old Blood and Old Guts; and, though not yet at the point where they were prepared to desert Resurgius and join the mutineers, they were bridling at the idea of retreat, and felt that attack, feet first, tooth and nail, was the only course. Resurgius' only thought was to hold as many of them together as he could, and get them to safety, so that, at some future date, they might make a comeback, a Risorgio-pimento.

The fact that they had shed themselves of the small force under Furius, which had attacked them, had only served to confirm Old Blood and Old Guts in the rightness of their stance. They forgot, almost instantly, that it had been Resurgius' counterattack which had saved them. Instead of leaving, they posted guards and held a victory celebration.

Meanwhile, Furius gave orders that six thousand Shrike-Troopers were to go ahead of her main body, circle round Old Blood and Old Guts' camp and, camouflaged as Birnam Wood, were to secure Small Hill on the far side of the mutineers' camp and wait for three blasts on her Moog, and then attack. First she would wipe out these mutineers, and then she'd go after Resurgius himself. She was already

211

beginning to repent having sent for Publia, because she saw now that Resurgius had no intention of making for the Pink House, as she had thought, but was indeed, in complete retreat. It would be a shame if Publia, whom Furius now knew to be close by, should run into Resurgius and defeat him, and get all the credit, when she herself had done all the dirty work.

It was a minor misfortune of her plans, that her camouflaged Shrike-Troopers on Small Hill were spotted by two camp-following Cunnies of the mutineers, who had climbed the hill to pick raspberries and had begun to pull apart one of the Shrike-Troopers, who looked for all the Universe like a raspberry bush. Things might have gone badly for these camouflaged Shrike-Troopers, but luckily Furius at that moment sounded three blasts on her Moog and the full attack was on.

Within minutes, Furius was able to proclaim herself the victor. It must be said, however, that of some ninety Dongs who were killed, only two were found to be wounded in their split infinitives, the rest having stood in their ranks and fought to the death like the fighting fools that they were, feet first, tooth and nail.

Old Blood Castratus was found, rigor mortis already setting in—it had been coming on for years—in a running position, face down, his old blood indicating a wound in the left cheek of his split infinitive.

Old Guts Cunnilingus was found in a similar position some yards away, but without a mark on him. An autopsy showed that he had swallowed a sunbeam up his arsehole, a lucky shot, even for an expert markswoman with a ray gun.

By the time that Resurgius got the sad news of the fate of the mutineers, he had already taken his remaining force deep into the Pocono Mountains, fully aware that he himself was being pursued. For the fact was that Typhus and

Scrofula, two of Furius' more bloodthirsty lieutenants had been dispatched to go on ahead to Resurgius' camp and keep an eye on him. But, when Resurgius decamped and started into the Poconos, these two, seeing that his force was terribly diminished, decided that, instead of reporting his actions, they would themselves overtake and capture him. Unfortunately for them, they did succeed in overtaking him, for their Shrikes were fresh and his Dongs were tired; but instead of the defeat which they had expected to administer, Resurgius rallied, faced them, and utterly routed them, sending them in great disarray back to Furius, who bit off their ears for cowardice. It has always been difficult for generals and historians to explain the twists and turns of fate. The more intelligent among them have insisted that the explanations of historical events be left to the narrative poets.

This strange success, however, turned out to be Resurgius' final ruination in the field, because it once again inspired his Dongs to fight. Now a large group of the more militant Dongs forcibly compelled their captain, one Erectus Custard, to lead them back upon the advancing army of Furius, which was exactly what the latter was eager for; the reason being that her Shrikes had begun to talk openly about the situation, saying that the honor of this war was reserved for she who would come and put some backbone into these slinky-spined troops and thus put an end to this war, which was costing everyone a pretty penny.

Furius, therefore, was eager to fight a decisive battle. So when, within an hour, she came upon Captain Erectus Custard and his Dongs, she was happy to supply him with the material for his last stand. (The Battle of Custard's Last Stand was fought in the late afternoon of Monday, Mae 20, 3000. Captain Erectus Custard and his complete compliment of Dongs were wiped out in this, the last important encounter of the Sex War.)

When Resurgius was brought word of Custard's Last Stand, his great green myopic eyes, magnified behind his hornrims, filled with tears. "The Establishment has proven too strong for us," he said, "and I, even in my Super-suit, have proven myself too weak to challenge it." He looked out on the draggled, mangled fifty-odd Dongs that he had left at his command and said, "Well, boys, let's call the whole thing off, shall we?"

They were too tired to answer.

For several days in his escape, Resurgius managed to keep just ahead of the advancing armies of Furius and Publia, which were vying with each other to strike the coup de grace.

On Thursday, Mae 23, 3000, Resurgius and his remaining Dongs came within view of the great spires of the LaMer Turnpike. There they disbanded, and, changing into the gray flannel business suits of Mize, two every hour, began to hitch rides from passing commuters into the city, where they took the long underground ride back to the LaMer Turnpike in surreptitious fashion, so that they might not be recognized as revolutionary Dongs, and in such circuitous manner returned to the Maidenform Brassiere Factory.

Resurgius, like a good captain, was the last to arrive.

"Well," said Beth, as he came up to her, shrinking inside his Super-suit, on shaky, if powerful-looking plastic legs, and hoping for a word of kindness with which to soothe his wounds of the spirit, and shame.

"You've certainly made a botch of it, haven't you?"

Debilitated, he looked back at her. "Frankly, my dear, I don't give a damn," he said, turning his eyes away from her protuberant boobs.

Was this, then, the death of the Dongs?

214

12

THE ETERNAL TRIANGLE

"Maybe Dongs really *are* inferior," Beth went on, dressing Resurgius down. "I never really believed it, but I'm beginning to now. How could you let a fool like Furius chase you back here to me with your dong between your legs?"

"She scared me. There were too many of them, all hen-pecking me. I was bloody with bites. They reminded me of my family, whom I couldn't stand—my aunts, my mother," Resurgius said.

"We've all got families. That's no excuse."

"I had to retreat; I couldn't engage that many Shrike-Troopers; my Dongs would have been cut off."

"Better that they had, than to come back here so shamefully, and dressed as Mize at that. For Cripe's sake, take off that lipstick! It doesn't go with your five-o'clock shadow."

"We had to disguise ourselves," said Resurgius, wiping the Maxine Factor stain from his lips, "otherwise we would have been picked up and thrown into a Boys Town detention camp, because we ain't heavy."

"Oh, what a weakling!" Beth cried impatiently. "How could I have been such a fool as to bet on you—a skinny little twerp in a plastic muscle-suit! Say," she added apprehensively, "you weren't followed, were you?"

"For Cripe's sake, no," he said, "I'm sure I wasn't."

"Well, this looks like the end of my political career. I'm shit on a stick," Beth soliloquized.

"Well, what about me?" asked Resurgius. "Don't you even have a kind word for me, after all I've been through? I did it all for you, you know."

"For *me*; that's a laugh!"

"You'd have been happy enough if I had won."

"But you didn't, you dumb Dong! You lost. Go on, get out of my sight, you loser, you musclebound piece of plastic, you skinny-necked intellectual brat! I've got some plans to make." At which, Beth's green eyes turned red with calculation, and Resurgius walked away, cursing his fate.

A few minutes later, he knocked on the door of the corset room.

"Who's there?" came the mellifluous, estrogen-loaded voice of Miz Mandalay.

"'Tis I, Resurgius, the great failure," said our hero in a sad voice.

The door flew open and the Amazonian Miz Mandalay stood looking down at him with big tears of joy and love squirting from her beautiful violet plastics.

"Oh, Resurgius!" she cried. "I had begun to think that you were lost in the Kloud and had become part of the babble of spacetime and I should never see you again." She threw her arms about his gigantic shoulders, and planted a dozen kisses all over his face, incidentally getting his lipstick on her cheek.

Resurgius was amazed by this Amazonian reception, though he wouldn't have been, had he been wiser in the ways of Mize, whose love is a process of incubation that, after months of stillness, bursts forth with a hearty cry.

"Oh, darling!" was that cry.

Taking her arms from his shoulders, Resurgius stepped back dizzily and looked at her.

"I was seeking more of the consolation of philosophy than of physiotherapy," he said, "but I never expected anything like this. Am I mistaken, or . . . do you love me?"

"I love you, Resurgius!"

"But I am a defeated Dong. I have no future to offer you."

"All the more reason for me to feel as I do, for I thought you were dead, and that made me suffer, and I had never suffered before, and I found it a rather pleasurable business: and now, because you return, as you say, a defeated Dong, you need me in a way that could not have been had you returned triumphant. Oh, my poor, dumb, defeated Dong, how you stir me with your failure! How my heart did sing at the news of your every defeat!"

"And yet you say that you love me?"

"By sun and candlelight!"

"Would you—would you mind explaining a little? Not that I don't feel highly gratified at the fact of your failed logic and increased love, but—"

"Of course, my poor, dearest Dong. But don't you see? No, of course you don't. A Miz understands these things. But it is only that, when you left, I thought you a worm; but it was possible that you might win, and return as a conqueror worm, to my dismay. We were enemies, officially, when you left. If you had returned a conqueror, it should have been I that you had conquered. But this way, with you defeated, I can imagine myself beginning a life with you; for I shall resign and we shall go to some satellite island and begin life anew as equals. Or I, a *little* superior, having come down in the world for your sake. And I will have you Resurgius, for you've tickled my fancy."

So saying, Miz Mandalay giggled, blushed, and began once again to plant kisses on Resurgius' spectacled face. Soon she had pulled him into the corset room and down upon a stack of panty-girdles, where they exploded into action.

"Oh my dear Mandalay," panted Resurgius, "all the time I was away at war I could think of nothing but the incredible softness of your behind."

"And for my part," panted Mandalay in reply, "I could think of little else but the incredible plastic hardness of your codpiece. You are my sex object!"

"And you are mine!"

"And you are mine!"

"Enough!" cried Beth, whose demeanor had returned to that of Miz Bet, and who suddenly stood in the doorway which, in their haste, our lovers had neglected to close. She had been looking for Resurgius; for, once her temper had cooled, her knickers had heated up. But now were again thoroughly frozen.

"Look at him!" Beth cried in the dramatic third person. "Regard this weak and treacherous Dong in whom I have placed a Cunnie's hope! See how he uses me! Or should I say, uses my enemy! I placed my faith in him to give me power and he has failed! Still, my physical attraction for him has kept me as loyal as I know how to be, which I must admit isn't very loyal. But still! And now this knickerknocking! If he thinks he's going to make a fool of me with another Cunnie, he's mistaken. He'll pay! He'll pay! I swear he will! This is it!" And she stalked off down the hall, her spiked heels clicking like hammers of revenge.

"She's pretty pissed," said Miz Mandalay. "You'd better go after her. She might do something we'll all regret."

"Oh, she'll chill out," said Resurgius.

"You mean calm down?"

"Yes. If she'd been nicer to me this might not have happened."

"Yes it would, inevitably. Passion is hot—but sometimes cold, fire and ice."

Upon leaving Resurgius and Miz Mandalay, Beth went directly to her private office in the old zipper room, and set into motion a plan which she had had half formulated before Resurgius' return, and which seemed to fall into a complete form with her discovery of Resurgius' sexual betrayal. Not only had her plan to seize supreme power been wrecked by Resurgius' military ineptitudes, as she saw them, but her sexual pride had been injured, and revenge was uppermost in her mind. Thus it was that, in a fit of blind rage, she tapped out the following message to Edgahoova, using her personal, F-phone:

Dear Jaye:

You are so right. Dongs are monsters at heart. It's true—in case you might have heard it—that my heart betrayed me, and I almost fell for Resurgius with a real plough—but not like the superplough that I've always had on you, dear Jaye.

You must believe me when I tell you that when I dropped out of sight nearly six weeks ago, I did it for you. You see, Jaye, I had a plan, and I knew that you wouldn't O.K. it, because it would put me in great danger, and you wouldn't want your special curvy Cunnie-wunnie in danger, I know.

I had met this Resurgius when he came to me on a crave call, when he was a stud. I discovered that he was the leader of a plot to overthrow the government. It was then that I decided to sacrifice myself, if need be, to save you and our blessed ovarian government from overthrow.

Naturally, I could trust no one, for he has spies every-where. So I took it upon myself to pretend to befriend him, fall in love, and run off with him. You see, I was playing a dangerous game and taking great risks for our Motherland.

Well, he has a strong mind, powerful persuasiveness, and large muscles, and it wasn't long before I found myself in his power—under his spell, I might almost put it. He is such a force for evil, as you must know.

But my head has cleared! Won't you take your little Cunnie-wunnie back into your giant lioness heart? You know that it has always been you for me. I've made a fool of myself. But I'm still your little playmate. Remember?

And now I'm ready to complete the job that I set out to do. Here's my plan: If you'll welcome me back into your good graces, I'll tell you where Resurgius is hiding.

Only—naturally, I have to take some care to my fu-ture—I require that you reply to this proposition on Public Say-screen, and that you make a public declaration about me, the gist of which should be: that you have word that I'm safe, and am soon to be released back to my duties by the rebel Dongs. Also, that you have confirmed that I am inno-cent of any wrong-doing, as indeed I am, unless it is a crime to be hypnotized and misused, and abused. Upon seeing this on Say-screen, you will within minutes receive word from me of Resurgius' whereabouts.

Hanging my hopes upon this thin thread, as well as upon the steel girder which I know your love to be, once given, and looking forward to our loving reunion, I am, as always,

Your Miz Bet

"It isn't much," Beth thought, pushing the activation button of the direct-line writer, "but it's all I've got. If horrid old Edgahoova's still as crazy about me as she was, she'll go for it. I might have my old job back by tomorrow. Oh, but Ugh! How I hate the thought of having her big paws on me again, pushing my head into her hairy bosom. I feel so different since the operation, kind of pro-fem. Eeek!"

Indeed, these thoughts greatly depleted her hope of re-establishment.

She turned on the Say-screen in time to catch the last part of her favorite soap opera, *The Killing of Brother Georgette*. While she waited for Edgahoova's reply, she sang sadly to herself:

"He was my Dong
But he done me wrong . . ."

At this very moment, Edgahoova was discussing Miz Bet's message with Furius who, fresh from battle, was soaking in a marble tub, a Pink Dongly with a banned plastic straw, resting on its wide edge.

"This ought to convince you if nothing else has," said Furius. "Can't you see through that transparent piece of ass? Can't you read between the lines?"

"I'm not exactly stupid, Furius," said Edgahoova. "I didn't work my way up to the top of the heap, Queen of the Mountain, Mistress Miz of the Pink House, by being dumb, you know. I've got plenty of animal cunning, if not brains, plus a law degree from Harvest. I'm a politician."

"Sure you have, Chief, you're from Newark, originally, aincha? Down Neck? I never thought different. But where that Miz Bet is concerned—well—"

"O.K.," said Edgahoova, "I've still got a crush on Miz Bet, but I can read too. But that's up to me. I'll decide what to do with Miz Bet later. But right now, let me give you a good example of the cunning that has made me great."

"Fire away, Chief," said Furius, sponging her muscular arms.

"Well, it's clear that Miz Bet is now disposed to do as I order, regardless of whatever else she's done to date, right?"

"Right! No doubt about that part of it, she's scared now, and has obviously turned against Resurgius."

"O.K. So let's extract a high fee for our good will, false though it may—and I say *may*—be. I've got to see her before I make up my mind about that."

"But what's the fee, Chief?"

"Well, if she tips us as to where Resurgius is hiding, and we get there and clean the place out, we're going to find Miz Mandalay. Now I don't want that liberal dame in my hair ever again. I want complete control of Atalanta. Ain't that what we all lust for? Actually, I'd like to have her bumped, one way or the other. But there's bound to be too much public notice on Resurgius' capture. It's a touchy situation. Something might go wrong if we bumped her then and there, and later it'd be even harder to get away with."

"You got a point, all right," said Furius. "But how're we gonna get rid of her?"

"That'll be the price we ask of Miz Bet—the price of that clean slate she wants."

"Say, Chief, that's a great piece of cunning. How'll we work it?"

"You'll see. Miz Bet's an experienced diplomat. She'll get the message."

And, suddenly, there it was: The Message!

Beth leaned forward in anticipation. An announcement had just been made that Jaye Edgahoova was to speak next. And there she was now, on Say-screen, Jaye Edgahoova herself.

"My gentle Mize," she began. "I have requested Say-screen time for the purpose of bringing you up to date on the conditions prevailing in Atalanta during this time of Dong erection.

"As you may know, our great and good military leaders, the great Publia and the immortal Furius, have today completely routed the Dong army which has threatened our happy way of life, and which was commanded by the infamous Dong, Resurgius. A Dong-count shows that many millions of Dongs were killed, whereas our fine Shrike-Troopers suffered no more losses than a few red tips from their longer fingernails. Of course, these things must be expected. Sacrifice is a part of war. It is the price you pay for our feminine freedom. As Abby Lincoln once said, 'Better dead than left ignored.' And in the words of the immortal Wilma Shakehips, author of 'Omelet' and 'Queen Leer,' 'The poor are sad because they are good. Therefore, take heart!' Ah, yes, inspiring words from the Immortal Bardess of Avon Calling. Let us heed them!

"Yes, the broken fingernails will grow back in a new burst of freedom. And when they do, we shall paint them in the colors of Atalanta's flag—feet first, tooth and nail! Now then, let's get down to cases.

"It is an unfortunate fact that Resurgius himself escaped capture, but it appears, even so, that he has come to the end of his ugly, male-factions.

"Allow me to elaborate. No doubt many of you have wondered about the strange disappearance of Miz Bet, one of my top aides. The fact is, six weeks ago I sent Miz Bet on a most hazardous mission. Her purpose: to infiltrate Resurgius' secret headquarters. And now my foresight and planning has borne fruit.

"I have, only a short time ago, received information as to the state of affairs in Resurgius' hideaway.

"It is tragic news.

"Our reports indicate that Resurgius, the infamous Dong leader, and the charismatic Miz Mandalay, whom you all know, and who it now appears was the victim only of a staged—I repeat, *staged*—kidnapping, and is in fact a spy and a traitor, and has been, in fact, Resurgius' accomplice and consort, have died in a suicide pact, directly resulting from Resurgius' defeat.

"It troubles me not a little to be forced to report that Miz Mandalay, formerly a leading member of the Univacual Council, has died in dishonor. But she died before she could do any more harm, and perhaps that's as well. Guten Abend, and as we Atalantans always say when toasting a cheerie event—not Cheers, not Prosit, but Up Yours!"

"So," said Beth to herself, turning off the Say-screen, "that's what the old devil asks of me, is it? Well, that seems like a pretty fair deal to me. She did clear me, pretty much, and that's a good sign. And he was my Dong, and he did do me wrong. And I hate that super bitch Mandalay anyway. But she died before she could do any more harm, Edgahoova said. That means I'd better work fast. Let's see, how shall I do it?"

Just then Resurgius' top remaining Dong Commander came jogging up the hall on powerful thighs and blistered feet, and pounded on the door. She pulled it open.

"I'm looking for Resurgius," he said.

"Is it about that Edgahoova speech that was on just now?"

"Yeah."

"Don't tell me you fell for that," said Beth. "You Dongs will believe anything."

"What do you mean?"

"That's exactly what Edgahoova's trying to do. She's trying to turn us against each other. You let me handle this. I'll tell Resurgius about it when he wakes up; he's sound asleep, poor Dong, exhausted from the war. You go back and tell everybody to calm down."

"But—"

224

"Do as I say, unless you want me to report you to Resurgius."

"Well—"

"Go on, now. Everything'll be ultra."

Looking unsure, the Dong turned and trotted back on powerful thighs and tender feet in the direction from which he'd come, which was Nowheresville.

"I have to act fast," thought Beth. "I know. I've got it. With a Spartacus snake I made him a leader, and with a Spartacus snake I'll poison him."

Beth ran to the kitchen—she was an excellent cook—rustled up two plates of green spaghetti with clam sauce, placed a little green asp in each plate, covered it, and took it into the hall, where she came upon a passing Dong, and, giving him the tray, told him to take it to Resurgius in the corset room and asp no questions.

> "He was my Dong
> But he done me wrong . . ."

she sang, walking away, and dreaming of reinstatement.

"Say, that looks good," said Resurgius, taking the tray from the Dong, "It's my favorite, green spaghetti and clam sauce. Wow, I sure did work up an appetite!"

"Me too," purred Miz Mandalay. "I'm starved."

Fortunately for them both, Resurgius, who had never mastered the art of Italian eating (by which we mean the use of spoon and fork and the winding up of spaghetti), and had been in the habit of feeding himself spaghetti with his fingers, as babies eat Gerber food, reached into his dish and, by chance, pulled an asp out by its tail.

"What's this?" he said. "This spaghetti squirms about as if it were alive. Perhaps it hasn't been cooked enough."

"I should say not," said Miz Mandalay, who had never been into a kitchen in her life. "Why they haven't even cut its head off. See, its tiny eyes are blinking."

"Nonsense," said Resurgius. "Spaghetti doesn't have eyes. It's made of whole food paste."

"It does so have eyes," said Miz Mandalay, "and a little forked tongue too, judging by the one you're holding."

Resurgius raised the thing up higher to see. He focused his hornrims.

"Cripes!" he cried. "That's not green spaghetti, that's a snake!"

Letting go of the tail-end of the little asp, he knocked Mandalay's plate from her hand, and dumped his own, and began stomping all over the squirming green stuff. Fortunately, he had not removed his hobnail boots while making love (he needed traction)—this was not inconsideration on his part; Mandalay simply hadn't given him the chance— and now the hobnail bottoms went to work chopping up snakes and spaghetti alike.

"I don't know which is which," he cried, in slight hysteria, "but I'll kill all of it. This dish'll be fit to eat before I'm done."

And indeed, he made a mincemeat of the whole mess. When he was done he flopped down next to Miz Mandalay on a stack of corsets, his giant plastic pectorals heaving.

"This could only be the work of one person," said Mandalay.

"Beth!" cried Resurgius.

"Hell hath no fury," said Mandalay proudly.

Five minutes later Resurgius had Beth arrested and thrown into the corset room, bound and gagged.

From now on, Resurgius and Miz Mandalay agreed, she was to have Beth's place in the cup next to Resurgius on the majestic bra.

"O, betrayal!" Resurgius cried, dumping his muscular, plastic buttocks into his cup. "O, treachery!"

"Alas," said Miz Mandalay, climbing into the cup next to his, "you must always remember, my great plastic hero, that hell hath no fury like a Cunnie scorned—and that might one day include me, my love. Circumstances are Fortune, my great muscled Cookie."

13

THE PINAFORE PAPERS

For Resurgius, Beth's attempt to murder him was the last straw.

"This revolution business is too much for me," he said later that night. "I just wish I could go off to the dark side of the moon and lead a quiet, meditative life."

"You're just tired," Miz Mandalay soothed. "You've been through hell."

"To hell and back," Resurgius said stoically.

"My hero," Miz Mandalay commented, squeezing his thigh.

"Mand—may I call you Mandy?"

"Yes, dear Dong, but how about Amanda, a name I always loved? Isn't it a fairy tale name? Doesn't it mean amorousness, affection, in short, love?"

"Would you consider giving up all this—Amanda—this ugly political life, I mean; this life of political monkey-hood—and running off with me to a desert planet, where it would just be thee and me and the drifting meteorites, the shooting stars?"

"Well, dear Dong, I do so hate to see you give up all that you've fought so hard for in the recent war; but, naturally, my love, whither thou goest, I will go. In the face of love, the life of politics seems but putrid trash. After all, as Jaye Edgahoova might say, politics is nothing but the profound entertainment of the people. I am no longer that interested in entertaining the people. I am in love, and therefore selfish; and perhaps that is the best way to be; to be an individual following his or her bliss. At least, minding my own business, I won't be doing them any harm, poor devils—and let them mind theirs. I often wonder why they do what we tell them to. We are no better than they are. If you cut us, do we not bleed?"

"Because they're afraid to think for themselves. Because they mix us up with their ideals."

"It's really quite sad. The herds of beasts must have a leader, I guess."

"Then you'll go with me?"

"Anywhere, anytime."

"Tomorrow morning, to the moon. From there we can get the shuttle on to Jupiter or Europa."

"It'll be like an old-fashioned honeymoon."

"Let's start tonight. The honeymoon part, I mean."

"Oh, you! Sugarplum."

But in the morning Resurgius had a change of heart. A good night's sleep, prefaced by a vigorous exercise of his sensitized, pumped-up codpiece, had restored his vitality, and once again he felt ready to conquer the Universe.

"I can't give up now," he said to his beloved Amanda, a spoonful of Coco-Puffies at his lips, "I have a responsibility to all the hard-beset Dongs of this world, who look up to me as a symbol."

"That's true, dear," she said. "Now eat your breakfast."

"If I were to quit now it would be like condemning them to another thirty years of slavery."

"It would have that effect."

"But won't you mind not going on our trip to the moon, and then shuttling on to Jupiter or Europa?"

"Resurgius, I knew that you didn't mean what you were saying. You were exhausted."

"I sure was, but I feel great now. Will you help me draw up a plan of action? I don't know how I'm going to do it yet, but I swear I'll think of some way of taking the Univacual Council away from Edgahoova, getting back the Pink House, and putting her on Pluto, where she belongs, just as the French once put Napoleon on Elba in ancient times."

"I'm afraid you might have to wait a while to do that, dear. You have too few Dongs to your name."

"Can't you—the great Miz Mandalay—go and reclaim your position?"

"You know perfectly well that that's impossible under the present circumstances. Edgahoover's branded me a traitor, publicly, and as long as *she's* the government, her accusation is true. I am a traitor, to *her* government. And don't forget, the Shrike-Troopers are scouring the country for us."

"I guess you're right," said Resurgius. "But there must be some way."

"We'll just have to wait, and build up a new army. My mother used to say that the shortest wait of all, is the wait for stupidity."

"Golly, that's a thought!"

But just then a Dong-trooper came into the padding room where Resurgius and Miz Mandalay were having stirred eggs, having finished their CoCo-Puffies.

"General-Admirable Resurgius," he said, "I have been instructed to tell you that big news is exploding all over the Say-screen. I have been instructed to request you to view this news, as it might be of great importance to our cause. Thank you, sir," he said snappily, and left, clicking his worn-down heels.

230

"What can that be?" said Amanda, turning in the Say-screen. She got a picture of Sandra Van Orchid, the renowned journalist, then turned up the volume.

Sandra said: "The whole Edgahoova regime has been shaken to its foundations by Daniela Illbird's revelations. Illbird, a member of the staff of the highly secret Strategic Force for Starvation, Death, Destruction and the Atalantic Way, a think tank, has revealed all; admitting that she has been married, illegally, to a Dong for several years. She is quoted as saying, 'I just got sick about what we've been doing to the poor Dongs.' Illbird has also made public many top-secret documents, which she calls the Pinafore Papers. These papers reveal deep and widespread corruption in the government. Surprise! Surprise! Who'd of thunk it?

"One document, a communiqué sent by General Furius to the Pinafore, and marked top-secret, reveals that General Furius' aunt, a Miz named Thickneck, was awarded the contract to build The Great Wall of Furius through her niece's instigation. General Furius herself received a considerable rake-off of taxpayer money, and so did Jaye Edgahoova. Such revelations as this are causing a tremendous public outcry against the current government (there's always another one), which, I hope my viewers will recall, I have always opposed. Mobs are roaming the streets chanting such tags as FRY FURIUS and HANG HOOVA! So far, there has been no comment from the Pink House. But, as I said, it is certain that the government of Jaye Edgahoova has been rocked to its foundations."

"This is it, Resurgius!" cried Amanda. "This is our *deus ex machina*!

"How?"

"*How*! Oh, I guess Mize think faster than Dongs. Don't you see? The people are ready for us. All we have to do now is to physically assume control. I have a marvelous record as a reformer. I've passed the only liberal legislation in this country since the Great Succession."

"You mean that one that gave all government employees a raise?"

"That one and many others—like that one that requires all Mize who own states to pay at least one bobbit a year in taxes. But never mind that! Stick to the point! I'm a reformer and everyone knows it. It was Edgahoova who blackened my good name, and now that the public knows what she is, they'll love me again, just like always, like Julius Caesar's. I've still got a legal claim to power, and I tell you Atalanta is ready for reform. If I assume power with you at my side, they'll accept you as my co-ruler, I know they will. We'll make it a real heterosexual government. We'll be equal partners!" Her delight compelled her into song:

> "Mize and Dongs together
> Me and Resurgius too—
> We'll trip the light fantastic
> On you, and you, and you!"

"O.K., but how'll we get to the Pink House?"

"I've already got that figured out. It's really easy. The balloon you used to kidnap me is still on the roof, isn't it?"

"Yeah. It's deflated, but it only takes a minute to blow it up. But that's no good; everybody knows about that balloon now, and Edgahoova's Shrike-Troopers'll shoot it down as soon as they spot it, and you have to admit that it's pretty noticeable."

"True enough," said Amanda, frowning. Then she grinned. "I've got it! We'll disguise it as an advertisement for that Old Roman Botula Sausage. All we'll need is some brown paint, and maybe a little black for the burnt part."

"Mandy, you're a genius! But how'll we get passed the guards at the Pink House?"

232

"We only have to worry about the guards on the roof, and I know all of them. They're a great bunch of gals."

"Okay," said Resurgius, "let's fly."

In no time at all, Resurgius, Amanda, three of Resurgius' best Dongs, all former gladiators, and the still bound-and-gagged Beth, were soaring toward Martha, D.C., and the Pink House.

Resurgius' Dongs had done a good job of painting the balloon. It was no longer the same old golden condom, but was now a crisply fried sausage that looked good enough to eat.

"We can be there in an hour," said Resurgius, "as the sausage flies."

"Oh, Resurgius," Amanda cried, "it's all so thrilling. As soon as we seize power, let's have a darling little Accidental, so that the people can truly think of us as the old fashioned First Family."

"Right, my Mandy, but I'll be pretty busy."

"Oh, we can always make time for love—between important meetings and things. There are lots of closets."

Resurgius was right, as usual. In less than an hour they came down over the roof of the Pink House. And Mandy was right too, for the guards cheered when they saw her, and cried:

"Why it's Miz Mandalay come home to us!"

"And I'll never leave you again, my darlings," she cried, tears squirting from her plastics and streaming down her cheeks. "And I want you all to meet Resurgius; he's my Dong."

"Is he safe?" asked one doubtful Shrike.

"He's a good Dong, believe me, dear. Now if you'll excuse us, we have work to do. We are going to fundamentally change this Universe."

Resurgius ordered that Beth be removed from the wicker basket of the balloon and to be brought along. Then the little group descended to the Ovary Office.

They had arrived not a minute too soon.

When they entered the Ovary Office, they found Edgahoova and Furius desperately packing taxpayer money and treasury plates into two huge trunks.

"Going somewhere?" asked Resurgius.

When Furius saw him, she turned purple, made an animal cry, and charged him. Fortunately, with foresight, and a knowledge of their adversary, all the members of Resurgius' party had taken the precaution of wearing earmuffs, and it was only an earmuff that Furius succeeded in tearing from Resurgius' head. With one powerhouse blow, he succeeded in flooring the unfortunate creature, which he had always wanted to do.

Edgahoova stood aghast.

"You are under arrest in the name of our George Washington," said Resurgius. "Let me warn you that anything you say may be used against you."

"You can't arrest me," said Edgahoova, getting her wits back. *I* am the law."

"No, you're not," said Resurgius. "I am!"

"*We* are, dear," put in Miz Mandalay.

"You're not," said Edgahoova, "I am."

"Well, there's only one way to settle this," said Resurgius, "and that's with logic." So saying, he stepped up to Edgahoova and drove an iron fist into her belly. She doubled up and sank to the floor. He straightened his horn-rims.

"Well, darling," said Miz Mandalay, "I guess we know who the law is now, don't we?"

Following Resurgius' orders, the three Dongs assumed supervision over the Pink House staff, and had Edgahoova and Furius thrown into the basement dungeon where taxpayers were often tortured. Edgahoova was placed in the same cell with Old Lynda Johnson, who has been held for many years on charges of war crimes, preferred by one-time philosophess, Bertha Bussle. Upon getting acquainted, they immediately began to twist each other's arms. Poor Old Lynda was really tickled to have an arm to twist, just like the old days. She would have picked Edgahoova up by the ears if she hadn't been so fat. As it was, she did show off her scar.

Almost immediately, Miz Mandalay made a request for Say-screen time, and naturally, was granted it. She handled herself admirably, giving the impression that there was nothing more natural than that she should be in command of the government. Not a soul thought to doubt it.

She spoke first, with Resurgius seated beside her.

"Have no fear, my fellow Atalanteans," she said, "the Ship of State is sailing smoothly, for no one current official has the power to send her from her course. Atalanta shall not fail to carry us forward into a future as yet undreamed, where every soul, like the seed of a great oak, will grow and spread and shut the sun from the ground.

"But the future is here and now. Therefore, my Atalanteans, I officially proclaim this day, Mae 25, 3000, as Equality Day. From this day forth, Dongs are recognized as full citizens of Atalanta, with all the rights and privileges thereof.

"And now, I should like to introduce you to the new Co-leader of Atalanta, the great General-Admirable Resurgius, former leader of the Dongs!"

"I only wish to say, on this solemn occasion" said Resurgius, "that I'll work with Miz Mandalay here to do my best to bring all of you together and to heal the wounds inflicted by the late civil war. I hope to be the leader of *all* the people, not just the ones I like. And I promise you that I'll do everything I can to please every one of you out there, with charity for all. I thank you."

After their speeches, Resurgius and Mandalay waited in front of the Say-screen to see if the reviews would be good or bad.

Sandra Van Orchid, the first to comment, said, "Let's give these fighting liberals a chance."

Norma Postman said: "I'd like to debate Resurgius. He's got some interesting ideas."

Petite Hannabelle said: "They're gutsy!"

Generally, the reviews were very good, and the general public took the attractive young couple to its heart. It was Camelotian.

In short, they were in like Flynne.

14

THE NEW ORDER

Nobody thinks of drawin' the distinction
between honest graft and dishonest graft.
—George Washington Plunkitt

In the first months of Resurgius' and Miz Mandalay's Co-leadership, they pleased the public by instituting many reforms, such as warning the school crossing guards about taking the children's' lunch money, and preventing the Old Roman Botula Sausage Company from stuffing their product with cow dung.

Actually, Resurgius left most of the administrative things to Miz Mandalay, now affectionately known to the public as Handy Mandy. He had bigger fish to fry.

Most of his first days in office were spent in coming to terms with the Space-Pirates. He was now in a much better position to bargain with Blackbeard than he had been at the time of their last meeting, and could truthfully claim that she and her Space-Pirates had done very little to help his cause.

On the other hand, Blackbeard still had a copy of their written agreement, which Resurgius had signed when he was at a low point, and which, if made public—Resurgius shuddered to think of the consequences. Besides which, Blackbeard had begun to harass his government with small space snarls. She really did own him, lock, stock, and barrel.

"Well," Resurgius thought philosophically, "was there ever a political leader who wasn't owned by someone?" Finally, he acceded to every one of Blackbeard's original demands.

"After all," he consoled himself, "it's the taxpayers' money, not mine." But he couldn't help thinking: "Yes, but it could have been better, honest."

One of Blackbeard's original demands had been that Resurgius keep the war on the dark side of the moon going, so that her cousin, the banker, might take over the Offence Industries, ownership of which in her cousin's name was another of her demands, so that he, the cousin, might supply bombs and rockets for the war. This meant that Resurgius was forced, eventually, to enact new draft laws, for the army was running low again on soldiers. Also, it was troublesome having to dream up circumstances which could be used to explain Atalanta's continued involvement there.

He was also responsible for punishing the guilty and rewarding the innocent. Publia he had arrested and thrown into the dungeon with Edgahoova and Furius. Claudia he pardoned, for, as we have mentioned, she married the Village Smithy. Cossina, who had defected to his side during the war, he welcomed back to Martha, D.C., with a triumphal parade, awarded her the Atalanta Shtick, highest of all medals, and made her Chief of Staff, all of which goes to show that the difference between a dirty traitor and an illustrious hero is just the difference between winding up on the losing or on the winning side.

On June 25, 3000, Edgahoova and Furius tried to escape, Edgahoova succeeding and Furius dying in the attempt. What had happened was that Furius had called her naive young guard over and asked if she might whisper something in her ear. The poor Cunnie put her ear to Furius' mouth and found herself to be captive. Furius forced her to unlock her cell, then to free Edgahoova.

Apparently, there was then some argument about taking Miz Bet along, which argument Furius won, convincing Edgahoova that she could not trust Miz Bet. But the argument had wasted precious minutes. Several more guards had entered the cell block. While Furius went after these newcomers, Edgahoova slipped away. She has not been seen or heard of since, but for the persistent rumor that she is the mysterious leader of the Vigilante Libs, a radical political group based on the dark side of the moon.

As for Furius, this attempt failing, she tried again to escape, and this time was killed in the attempt, falling off her famous Brahma rocket nicknamed "Bull." The rocket itself had been bent in half due to her weight and clutching legs, and is now in a museum to show what happens to evil-doers: they spin in circles forever—unless they fall off.

Publia was brought to trial, and through the influence of Blackbeard, who was her second cousin once removed, she was given a suspended sentence on her charge of treason.

"All's well that ends well," she was heard to comment. Upon her release, she went back into show biz, which, if you'll remember, had been her first love, taking a job as a Dong impersonator in an All-Night Club.

15

RESURGIUS IN LOVE

Resurgius had only one other problem, and that was the question of how, what had come to be called "L'affaire Bet" by the public, should be handled.

Amanda had become an awful pest about this situation, for it was her most ardent desire that she and Resurgius should be married, that venerable institution now having been given once again the sanction of law. She wanted them to be the first First Family of the New Order, but how could this be done so long as Beth kept insisting from her cell in the Pink House dungeon that she was actually Resurgius' wife, and therefore the First Lady of the Land?

Resurgius cursed himself for ever having married her. He had only done so because she had made him feel gratitude toward her and had told him that it was love. Now, through Amanda's offices, he knew better.

Desperate, he summoned his top legal advisor, Attorney General Mitch Shyster, and his top spiritual advisor, The Reverend Billy Cracker.

"What shall I do?" he asked of them.

Attorney General Shyster replied:

"The marriage wasn't legal in the first place, for there was a specific law against the institution of marriage at the time, and, frankly, I sometimes wish you hadn't countermanded it."

"All right," said Resurgius, searching his conscience, "perhaps it wasn't legal in the eyes of the Law, but what about in the eyes of the Lord?"

"Ah kin only ahdvise yo, suh," said the Reverend Billy, "ta search out yo conscience. When yo sayed 'I do' didja mean it, or was yo bein' misguided by thah forces of Evil?"

"I think I was being misguided."

"Then they is no marriage."

"Golly, thanks a lot fellows—this is a great day for yours truly," said Resurgius. "But I'm still going to have to get rid of Beth or she'll always be in my hair."

"Let yo conscience be yo guide, my son," said the Reverend Billy.

Next day, Resurgius brought charges against Beth. He charged her with treason against the former government. Her epaulettes were torn from her shoulders and turned into heavy-duty mops. She was then exiled to Pluto, much as Napoleon had been exiled to Elba, to live a life of contemplation and regret.

Resurgius and Amanda enjoyed their nuptials later the same afternoon. Both died in office, Resurgius first, unfortunately, of toxic masculinity caused by his plastic muscle-suit with the big "R" on its chest, which turned out to be poisonous—and at his state funeral all that was left to observe was his skinny little body, his big head with its shock of auburn hair, his huge hornrimmed, thick-lensed spectacles, and a wan smile of victory. He had a right to his rictus, having put Dongs in their rightful place.

The beautifully embosomed Amanda died some twenty years later, having enjoyed two decades of a smashing superduper Univacual high life.

WOW!

CPSIA information can be obtained
at www.ICGtesting.com
Printed in the USA
BVHW031343281119
565023BV00004B/11/P